LEVIATHAN AND NATURAL LAW

Leviathan
and
Natural
Law

BY

F. Lyman Windolph

GREENWOOD PRESS, PUBLISHERS
NEW YORK

◄⦗ FOREWORD ⦘►

I HAVE been reading and thinking on the subject of politics for more than forty years. This book is the result. Aubrey recorded of Hobbes that "his contemplation was much more than his reading." Both of these ingredients have gone into the making of the book, but I cannot tell what the proportions are. On the one hand, I am as well aware as anyone that I have not originated a system of political philosophy and that most, perhaps all, of what I have had to say has been said or at least suggested before. On the other hand, I have tried to set forth my own opinions, from whatever source they may have been derived, and not to summarize or review the opinions of other men.

There is a sense in which it can hardly be denied that the book is timely. The days of my years have been keyed to momentous events. When my interest in politics began, most Americans were inclined to take for granted the merits of democracy and liberty, and to regard the nature of sovereignty and the problems of dual government as subjects of little interest or importance except in academic debate. Two world wars, the widely felt aspirations for some sort of international political organization that they have occasioned, and the sharpness of the issue between the democratic and totalitarian conceptions of the state have removed these questions from the lecture hall and the study, and have presented them with terrifying urgency for consideration in the market place. In discussing them in the text I have been concerned with first principles, not specific remedies, and

⟨ v ⟩

I have thought of myself as addressing general readers of intelligence and curiosity rather than professional scholars.

In the course of my reading and contemplation I recurred again and again to the disagreement between the political philosophers known as positivists and the adherents of natural law. The positivist insisted that in order to think clearly about political matters I must make a rigid separation between politics and morality—between things as they are and as I might conceive that they ought to be. The champion of natural law answered that such a separation was undesirable and, in any event, impossible. Natural law represented the common reason of mankind and was the only basis and justification of political forms. To this the positivist replied that natural law was "nothing but a phrase."

The positivist convinced me that if I wanted to understand the things that are Caesar's, I must first identify Caesar, note the inscription on the coin of the tribute and study the decree under which the tribute was imposed. He did not convince me that natural law was nothing but a phrase, but I was prepared to admit that it was not a political phrase. It seemed to me that the natural law philosopher was at his strongest when he declared boldly that his chief concern was not with politics but with morality, and at his weakest when he tried to point in both directions at once. His message to me was that when a man becomes a student of politics he does not cease to be a man, and that when I had completed my investigation of the things that are Caesar's, I could not escape from the obligation of inquiring how far they corresponded with the things that are God's.

In the end I came to believe that the issue between the competing schools was partly verbal, and that if I could act as moderator in a sort of round table discussion between, let us say, Aquinas and Hobbes, each of them would be compelled to make admissions that would at least narrow the apparent field of disagreement. Surely, I thought, I could get Aquinas to admit that a governor of Judaea once pronounced a sentence of death, that the sentence was carried out, and that the existence of an unlimited power to confiscate and condemn is one of the characteristics of political societies. Surely, I thought, I could get Hobbes to admit that both the imposition and the execution of this particular sentence were iniquitous. The undertaking appeared to be a formidable one: no less than to induce Leviathan to lie down with the Lamb. Nevertheless, I was resolved to make the attempt.

I had no trouble with Aquinas. The sovereign, he said, is "exempt from the law, as to its coercive power, since, properly speaking, no man is coerced by himself, and law has no coercive power save from the authority of the sovereign." In this sense, though of course not in the moral sense, "there is no man who can judge the deeds of a king." It would be hard to find a plainer acknowledgment of one of the fundamental tenets of positivism.

It will astonish some readers to know that I made a certain amount of progress with Hobbes. He had a lively faith in many dogmas in which I believe and in some in which I happen not to believe—e.g., the literal inspiration of the scriptures. He extolled "our naturall Reason" as "the undoubted Word of God," and laid down an elaborate series of precepts that the sovereign *ought* to observe. Failure to observe them constituted "a breach of trust, and of the Law of Nature." If the sovereign employed "a Publique Minister, without written Instructions what to doe," the minister was "obliged to take for Instructions the Dictates of Reason." A judge, presumably also uninstructed, was bound by natural law and must give judgment accordingly. In the case in Judaea Caesar had issued no instructions to his minister, and I found nothing in Hobbes that would require him to hesitate in denouncing the imposition of the sentence.

This, however, was as far as he was willing to go. I could not get him to denounce the execution of the sentence. In a state of nature all men were subject to the principles of natural law, but they had discovered that life in such a state was "solitary, poore, nasty, brutish and short." In order to avoid these disadvantages and to secure the inestimable advantages of safety and order, they had submitted themselves to the power of a sovereign. Thereafter their only duty was to obey. Judges and other "publique ministers" represented the person of the sovereign and their orders were his.

I can sum up my judgment of Hobbes in a single statement. He cared more about peace than about justice. This is a dangerous doctrine in any age. It is a fatal doctrine in the age in which we live.

What I regard as an even more fatal aberration has been given currency by certain modern writers, who have accepted the implications of Hobbes's political philosophy while rejecting his faith. He never doubted that men were endowed with the capacity to distinguish right from wrong, but held that they were prevented from acting on the distinction against the commands of the sovereign. The writers to whom I am referring suggest that the distinction itself has no relation to objective reality and depends on nothing more enduring than personal predilections. Truth is only the opinion that is fated to prevail.

I have dealt briefly with these doubts in the concluding chapter, and particularly with the views of Holmes, for whom, on most grounds, I entertain a warm admiration. I will say here only that if the doubts are well founded, the story of the fall of man is more tragic than we have hitherto been taught to believe. The fruit of the forbidden tree was only pretended fruit. The knowledge of good and evil was something more deadly than a curse; it was a mockery and a deception.

I have written this much, but the reader may still be uncertain why I have written the book. It has been truly said of Hobbes that he founded political positivism on the basis of natural law. Perhaps it might be said of me that I have reversed the process and have attempted to found a theory of natural law on the basis of positivism. That, at least, has been the course of my own thinking. I can claim nothing for it with confidence except the integrity that is inherent in every effort to clear the mind of preconceptions and prejudices and to reason with accuracy and candor. The conclusions as well as the method are mine. I have no means of knowing to what extent they will commend themselves to anyone else. However slight the justification may be, I must find what encouragement I can in the saying of Correggio with which Montesquieu brought to a close his preface to *The Spirit of Laws*: "And I also am a painter."

CONTENTS

1. THE THINGS THAT ARE CAESAR'S

Some man or group in every form of state
Has sovereign power to kill and confiscate.

THE THINGS THAT ARE CAESAR'S

THE primary fact in politics is the existence of the government. The lawmaker, the judge, the policeman, and the tax gatherer are representatives of the government who are familiar to all of us. Under one name or another they have been equally familiar in every civilized age. The first question in the catechism is not what the world is but who made it. In like manner the first question in the unwritten catechism of politics ought to be who made the government.

The orthodox answer to this question is that the sovereign made the government. After the fashion of catechisms this answer begets another question: who is the sovereign? The sovereign is that individual or group (whether large or small) possessing at a given time and in a given state absolute and unlimited power. A final question is thus presented: what is a state? A state is an independent political society consisting of an aggregate of sovereign and subjects.

The story of Robinson Crusoe may be regarded for political purposes as a parable in three parts. The first part is concerned with Crusoe alone on his island. The poet has caused him to say that he was monarch of all he surveyed and that his right there was none to dispute. This may be poetry but it is not politics. A man cannot be monarch over himself. Neither can he confer rights on himself.

In the second part of the story the coming of Friday converted a solitude into a society in which Crusoe, because he had a gun, possessed absolute power. Crusoe was sovereign in this society and he and his subject constituted a state. In the nature of the case Crusoe ruled his subject directly; hence he was the government as well as the sovereign.

Instead of shooting Friday, as he might have done, Crusoe assured him of protection and kind treatment so long as he behaved himself in a specified way. What happened was not the proposal of a contract but the publication of a charter. If Crusoe had afterwards revoked the charter and had shot Friday, his act would have been a sin but not a crime. On the other hand, if Friday had tried to kill Crusoe, the attempt would have been treason if it had failed and revolution if it had succeeded.

In the third part of the story the state was enlarged by the arrival on the island of a Spanish castaway and Friday's father. Thereupon Crusoe granted a limited authority to Friday in certain respects and to the Spaniard in certain other respects. Crusoe now had three subjects instead of one, but he was no longer more than a part of the government. Friday and the Spaniard had become parts of the government, serving at the sovereign's pleasure.

The distinction between the state and the government is of fundamental political importance. Whether it was known to Aristotle is a question about which scholars are not in agreement. At all events, it was much less easily apparent in the small Greek city-states with which Aristotle was acquainted than it is in those modern states in which the sovereign has published a written constitution announcing the creation of the government and enumerating and limiting its powers. A modern writer has said that "the government is the administrative agent of the state, *like the board of directors of a corporation.*" The comparison is helpful though not entirely accurate. If we apply it here, we may say that the Greek states were so small that the controlling stockholder was always also an important member of the board of directors, and that in the Greek democracies the stockholders and directors were the same persons—i.e., the whole body of citizens constituted the assembly.

A somewhat similar source of confusion exists in modern England because of the fact that the House of Commons, which is the body in which the sovereign power of the English people is organized, is also—and indeed for most purposes—simply a coordinate branch of the legislature. If we think of it in this latter capacity, we may say that the *government* of England is monarchical as to the King, aristocratic as to the Lords, and democratic as to the Commons; but when the House of Commons acts as the mouthpiece of the *sovereign,* both the King and the Lords must and do bow to its will.

The English system demonstrates that a state and its government are not always of the same kind. A sovereign individual may see fit to establish a popular government. On the other hand—as in the recurring figure known as "the man on horseback"—a national emergency may induce a sovereign group to confer all the powers of government on a single individual. History has shown that the latter combination is almost invariably unstable. Either the termination of the emergency results in a prompt withdrawal of the powers conferred or the individual on whom they were conferred conducts a revolution, overthrows the former sovereign and takes supreme power into his own hands.

The validity of what has been said depends on a proposition that may be expressed as follows: in every political society you must come at last to some power which is absolute, to which all other powers are subject, and which itself is subject to none. The possession of such power is sovereignty, and the person or body in whom it resides is sovereign. If this proposition is correct, we may dispose once and for all of criticism of the sort implied in the bitter and indeed dreadful saying attributed to a returned soldier that he had given up one of his legs but that the diplomats would not give up any of their sovereignty. If sovereignty is a prerogative, there are no words too bitter and dreadful with which to denounce it. If it is a fact, an injured aviator might say with no greater relevancy that he had given up one of his legs but that the scientists would not give up any of their law of gravity.

In the modern world the use of force, at least in the ultimate sense, is to be found only in the field of politics. In former times the church held courts, kept prisoners, and pronounced sentences of death. Therefore Maitland argued that the medieval church was a state. Be that as it may, neither the church nor any other voluntary group exacts obedience from its members today by the exercise or threat of physical force. On the other hand, you may disregard the directions of the policeman only at the peril of arrest. The sentences of the judge are executed by sheriffs and marshals. The legislator levies taxes and conscripts soldiers in time of war. The policeman, the judge, and the legislator are, however, no more than agents of the government acting under the forms of law. The government, like the centurion in the New Testament, is itself under authority, having soldiers and servants under it. Our question is not about the power (absolute in quality but limited in scope) that is exercised by the government, but whether, behind and outside the government, there exists sovereign power (i.e., power both absolute and unlimited) that can condemn and confiscate without a hearing and out of mere prejudice and caprice.

Most Americans will be tempted to remark that however the case may be in a dictatorship, the precise merit of a democracy is that the citizen is protected from the exercise of arbitrary power. The fallacy of this contention becomes apparent the moment we inquire by whom the democratic citizen is protected.

We are accustomed to enumerate the liberties that are enjoyed by the citizens of our own democracy. The people are to be secure against unreasonable searches and seizures. Cruel and unusual punishments are not to be inflicted. Accused persons are to be tried in accordance with the traditions of English liberty. If, therefore, the President of the United States were to proceed by arbitrary fiat against the lives or property of his political opponents, his act of usurpation would be declared void by a decree of the Supreme Court. In the case supposed, a right granted to citizens as the result of a corresponding limitation imposed on the executive would be protected by a power conferred on the judiciary. The sources of the right, the limitation, and the power are all to be found within the four corners of the Constitution of the United States.

But the power that made the Constitution yesterday can unmake it tomorrow. I am not referring to the ever present possibility of revolution, but to the orderly process of amendment reserved in the Constitution itself. Suppose a resolution to be introduced in Congress proposing a constitutional amendment empowering the President to proceed by information against political offenders, and to try and sentence them in the exercise of his sole discretion. Suppose this resolution to be carried by the requisite two-thirds majority in both houses of Congress. Suppose the proposed amendment to be duly ratified by the legislatures of three-fourths of the commonwealths. Suppose, finally, a sentence of death to be imposed by the President in strict accordance with the authority conferred upon him. To whom then would the threatened citizen look for protection? The answer must be that he could look nowhere for protection. The illustration may be objected to on the ground that no such amendment as the one suggested could possibly be adopted. This objection amounts to nothing except an expression of faith that a sovereign who has acted considerately in the past will probably continue to act considerately in the future. "And whosoever," as Hobbes observed with characteristic clarity, "thinking Soveraign Power too great, will seek to make it lesse; must subject himselfe to the Power, that can limit it; that is to say, to a greater."

I think there can be no escape from this logic or from the underlying fact that gives rise to it. If you live in a political society at all, some man or group can confiscate your property and forfeit your life.

The theory of the absolute sovereign is no older than Bodin, the French political philosopher of the sixteenth century, and comes to us by way of Hobbes and Austin. If the sovereign made the government, who made the sovereign? Hobbes (and after him Locke and Rousseau, though for very different purposes) professed to find the origin of the state in an original compact or covenant. According to Hobbes, this compact was irrevocably entered into among the people, and the sovereign, though not a party to it, was nevertheless created by it. According to Locke, the compact was conditionally made between sovereign and subjects, and the power given up by the contracting parties became vested in the community as a whole. According to Rousseau, the people contracted in some mysterious way both among themselves and also with the state that arose from the original contract. These theories led Austin to write tartly about "the conceit of an original covenant which never was made anywhere, but which is the necessary basis of political government and society." I share his sense of irritation. In the history of primitive peoples there is not a vestige of evidence that any of the supposed covenants was ever made. We must dismiss them all as dialectical devices from the imagined necessity for which the science of politics has been happily emancipated.

Bodin advanced a more realistic theory. Like Aristotle he begins with the family, but he goes a good deal further. I present his view not as a universal hypothesis that is capable of verification but as a piece of speculation more nearly in accordance with the known facts of history than any theory of contract. "Before there was either city or citizen," he wrote, "or any form of a commonwealth amongst men every master of a family was master in his own house, having power of life and death over his wife and children; but after that force, violence, ambition, covetousness, and desire of revenge, had armed one against another, the issues of wars and combats, giving victory unto the one side, made the other to become unto them slaves; and, amongst them that overcame, he that was chosen chief and captain, under whose conduct and leading they had obtained the victory, kept them also in his power and command as his faithful and obedient servants, and the other as his slaves. Then that full and entire liberty, by nature given to every man to live as himself best pleased, was altogether taken from the vanquished, and in the vanquishers themselves in some measure also diminished in regard of the conqueror; for that now it concerned every man in private to yield his obedience unto his chief sovereign; and he that would not abate any thing of his liberty, to live under the laws and commandments of another, lost all. So the words of lord and servant, of prince and subject, before unknown to the world, were first brought into use. Yea, reason, and the very light of nature, leadeth us to believe very force and violence to have given cause and beginning unto commonwealths."

Whatever the origin of sovereign power may be, its location at a given time and in a given state is always a question of fact. The science of morals is concerned with things as they ought to be. The science of law is concerned with things as they are supposed to be. The science of politics is an iron science and is concerned with things as they are. Therefore it is clear that when we speak of absolute power we have in mind a reality rather than a fiction—the actual power once exercised by the Czars of Russia and not the ostensible or legal power still attributed in formal documents to the English kings. Let me illustrate by two imaginary incidents that might have occurred in the course of my own lifetime.

The last of the Czars is walking with a companion on the terrace of one of his palaces. There is a sentry on the terrace who is acquainted with the person of the Czar and recognizes him. Of course the sentry is armed. The Czar approaches him and says, "Shoot this gentleman—he is a traitor," or perhaps just "Shoot this gentleman," without any explanation. What will the sentry do? I believe there can be little doubt that he will obey the order as readily as his predecessor would have obeyed a like order in the reign of Ivan the Terrible.

Now suppose the same incident to be repeated at Buckingham Palace during the reign of Edward VII. (I say Edward VII because he was a contemporary of Nicholas II, but I could go back much farther in English history and get the same result.) You know what the result is—there will not be any shooting. Instead the sentry will say something. We do not know exactly what this will be but we do know the substance of it. He will say, "That wouldn't be constitutional, your Majesty"—the best answer of all—or, "I couldn't do that except under orders from my colonel"—not as good an answer, but still a good one—or, "Has your Majesty seen the Court Physician recently?"—or something like that. It is possible, of course, that an exceptionally high-minded and courageous Russian might have refused to obey the command of the Czar, but if he had done so there would simply have been two victims instead of one—the order would have been carried out by other soldiers in the service of his master and he himself would have been executed for disobedience. On the other hand, if the British sentry had obeyed the order he would have been tried for murder and it is altogether likely that the King would have lost his throne.

The illustration of the two sentries does not furnish a complete description of sovereign power. There are things which no sane ruler, however inconsiderate, would venture to do—commands which could be issued and which, if issued, would be obeyed, but the execution of which would create an imprudent hazard of the inconvenience of rebellion or the fatality of revolution. It follows that sovereignty must be understood to refer to power either actual or potential—"irresistible force, not necessarily exerted but capable of being exerted." You may object that if potential power is to be considered, the existence of every state rests on the approval or at least on the acquiescence of the masses. Perhaps this is the meaning of the much debated saying of Aristotle that "in every government [state] the majority rules"—a saying which has been repeated in various forms by Burke and Savigny and which, if taken at its face value, might compel the admission that all states are democratic. The obvious rejoinder is that the sort of power we are talking about is the actual or presently potential power of an existing sovereign, and not the remotely potential power by which at some future time the sovereign may be overthrown. Ivan the Terrible executed a large number of his subjects. Probably he was not altogether sane, but we must suppose that even he realized that there might be one execution too many. We need not inquire what would have happened if he had issued a final and provocative order. The point is that, regardless of consequences, so long as whatever orders he issued would have been obeyed, he was the sovereign of Russia.

Considerations such as these have led some political philosophers to reject the definition of the state in terms of force and to attempt to define it in terms of will. The situation of the Czar and the sentry is obviously not exactly that of Crusoe and Friday. Crusoe had a gun and Friday did not. On the contrary, the sentry was armed and the Czar was not. Nevertheless, the sentry (and behind him the army and behind it the people) yielded as implicit obedience to the Czar as Friday yielded to Crusoe. It is said that they *willed to obey*, and that this act of will is the true basis of political forms. The issue here seems to me to be about words rather than things. No challenge is directed to our fundamental proposition about the all powerful man or group. I have seen somewhere a couplet, doubtless an imitation of the famous epigram of Pope, about the case of his Lordship and the dog—

"I am his Lordship's dog at Wrightham,
And whom he bids me bite I bite 'em."

You may begin as I do with his Lordship *bidding* the dog to bite, or you may begin with the dog *wanting* to bite when he has been bidden—in either case I think you will come to pretty much the same place in the end.

It has likewise been argued that "the real rulers of a

political society are undiscoverable." According to this theory Rasputin was perhaps the unidentified sovereign of Russia at a time when the elder J. P. Morgan was perhaps the unidentified sovereign of the United States. This is a modern instance of a very old argument. Plutarch quoted Themistocles to the effect that his son was the most powerful of the Greeks, since he gave orders to his mother, the mother gave orders to Themistocles, Themistocles gave orders to the Athenians, and the Athenians gave orders to the rest of the Greeks. The problem has been posed in another form and I state it only for the pleasure of bringing a lady to the center of the stage. If the Athenian assembly invariably followed the advice of Pericles and Pericles invariably followed the advice of Aspasia, who was the sovereign of Athens? "Is not this the vain and infinite search for causes of causes? The answer is plain. Successful persuasion is not sovereignty"—and to assert the contrary is to run the risk of having to declare that not Aspasia but the domineering mother of the lover of Aspasia's favorite slave girl was the true sovereign of Athens.

We have noted that the location of sovereign power in a given state and at a given time is never a question of law. It is likewise never a question of morals.

The Declaration of Independence proclaims that "all men . . . are endowed *by their Creator* with certain unalienable rights" and that governments derive "their *just* powers from the consent of the governed." The significance of these statements is to be found in the words that are here placed in italics. When men take up arms, protesting that they do so to defend rights with which they have been "endowed by their Creator" and to advance the "just powers" of government, they are not talking politics. They are saying in effect that to act as they propose is righteous and that to act otherwise would be base; and they are seeking approval of their conduct by the judgment of the "candid world" to which their declaration is addressed. We may speak of revolutions as political phenomena only in the way in which we may speak of miracles as natural phenomena. They lie outside the field of political philosophy, just as miracles lie outside the field of natural philosophy, and they are to be justified or condemned on moral and historical grounds.

When Thomas Jefferson composed the Declaration of Independence, he was a rebel in fact and a traitor in law. That he lived to become President of the United States was a result of the fact that the redcoats of King George proved in the end unequal to the task of dispersing the continentals of General Washington. If the event had been otherwise and the British ministry had been foolish enough to push its cases against the leaders of the colonists, Jefferson might very well have ended his life upon a scaffold. Had he done so, some British cynic might have been heard to inquire in what sense his right to life could be described as unalienable. The friends of Jefferson might have replied that posterity would remember him as a nobler figure than his executioner or than the sovereign whom his executioner served, and that there is a power in the universe whose judgments are more to be regarded than those of any earthly tribunal. These arguments are so weighty as to require consideration in a separate chapter. This much is certain, however —whether true or false, they would have been ineffective, so far as Jefferson himself was concerned, to mitigate the force or dull the edge of the descending axe.

2. THE THINGS THAT ARE NOT CAESAR'S

The sovereign gives commands. Let conscience tell
When subjects should obey and when rebel.

THE THINGS THAT ARE NOT CAESAR'S

THE dilemma that ensues when the commands of the sovereign come into conflict with the conscientious convictions of his subjects is as old as politics and almost as old as morality. It was presented by Sophocles in the scene in which Creon accuses Antigone of having violated the proclamation by which the rites of burial were denied to her brother.

CREON: Tell me, tell me briefly:
Had you heard my proclamation touching this matter?
ANTIGONE: It was public. Could I help hearing it?
CREON: And yet you dared defy the law.
ANTIGONE: I dared.

It was not God's proclamation. That final Justice
That rules the world below makes no such laws.

Your edict, King, was strong,
But all your strength is weakness itself against
The immortal unrecorded laws of God.

> They are not merely now: they were,
> and shall be,
> Operative for ever, beyond man utterly.

This is said with the passion and simplicity of poetry, and it cannot be said better. Nevertheless, the only *political* comment that it invites is the barren one that civil disobedience is a form of rebellion and that every rebellion must inevitably fail and be crushed or succeed as a revolution. Antigone is not interested in this aspect of the problem. She is not thinking about politics and she expressly admits Creon's power. She is thinking about *morality*.

In order to sit in judgment between her and Creon it is not essential to accept any particular system of moral philosophy. It is essential to admit only that the realm of morality exists independently of the realm of politics —that is, that one sort of behavior may properly be described as better or more virtuous than another and that the distinction does not depend on force. You may believe with St. Augustine that the source of the distinction lies in the will of a "God and Lord of all . . . in whose presence are the causes of all uncertain things, and the immutable patterns of all things mutable, with whom do live the eternal reasons of all these contingent chance-medleys, for which we can give no reason." You may adopt the utilitarian theory of Bentham and his followers, and profess to find the whole duty of man in so acting as to bring about, in the long run, the greatest happiness for the greatest number. You may content yourselves with the less ambitious statement of Pollock that there are "principles of conduct [which] are common to and admitted by all men who try to behave reasonably." For present purposes, you may even conclude with Holmes that "our test of truth is a reference to either a present or an imagined future majority in favor of our view." You may, in short, think of morality in any way you please except one—you may not agree with Plato's Thrasymachus, who sought to persuade Socrates that "justice is nothing else than the interest of the stronger." He did not succeed in convincing Socrates and he does not succeed in convincing me, although I think reflection will show that his view cannot be refuted by arguments such as may be made in deciding mathematical and scientific questions. The refutation rests at bottom on an act of faith. If you cannot make this act of faith, you may as well omit the rest of this chapter. The discussion is not worth reading because there is nothing to discuss. The issue between Antigone and Creon has simply disappeared. Nothing can be said on her behalf. Might and right have become interchangeable terms and *his* will is the only measure of *her* duty.

I have used the word *right*, and in so doing have suggested its opposite, *wrong*. No two words in the English language have been subjected to greater abuse and require more careful consideration before being put into circulation. If anyone, said Locke, "shall well consider the errors and obscurity, the mistakes and confusion, that are spread in the world by an ill use of words, he will find some reason to doubt whether language, as it has been employed, has contributed more to the improvement or hindrance of knowledge among mankind." The situation can hardly be as bad as Locke would have us believe, but it is bad enough to give us pause. For the moment let us leave Creon and Antigone confronting one another and attempt to define our terms. The attempt will illuminate, if it will not wholly resolve, the disagreement between them.

In modern English the adjective *right* is not used in a political or legal sense—i.e., it is sometimes a synonym of *righteous* but never of *rightful* in the sense of lawful. Our troubles begin with the noun. As moralists we may repeat the phrase of Jeremiah about the right of the needy, meaning a *claim* to performance or forbearance recommended by considerations of justice and mercy. But as citizens we may also quote the constitutional provision about the right of the accused to a speedy and public trial, and in so doing refer to a *power* possessed by the accused to require performance or forbearance by the government. According to Robert Frost,

"Home is the place where, when you have to go there,
They have to take you in."

It is likewise true that, under certain conditions, they have to take you in at the County Home, but the kind of compulsion is obviously not the same.

A political critic has remarked that there can be no objection to the use of an equivocal word when its different senses are plain and palpable, and has given as examples the word *light*, which sometimes means the contrary of *heavy* and sometimes the contrary of *dark*; and the word *duty*, which sometimes means a moral obligation and sometimes a tax on a commodity. The first illustration should serve to reconcile us to the use of the word *right* both as the contrary of left and as descriptive of an angle of ninety degrees. The force of the second illustration is, however, the reverse of that intended, since, as the Boston Tea Party demonstrates, a question may arise about the moral obligation of subjects to pay a tax on a commodity—that is, about their duty to pay a duty. The ambiguity here arises from the fact that the two meanings of the equivocal word, instead of being plainly and palpably different, are really related. One meaning, no matter which, has been derived from the other. One has been appropriated to the field of morals, the other to the field of law, and a contradiction instantly appears in any connection in which morality and the law find themselves at odds.

The confusion between moral wrongs and legal wrongs is at least as common as that between moral rights and legal rights. The maxim of the courts that the state (more accurately, the sovereign) can do no wrong was characterized by Hallam as "a prudent fiction"; but it is not a fiction whether prudent or otherwise. It is a truism, and what it means is that, in the very nature of the case, "there can be no legal right as against the authority that makes the law on which the right depends." To suppose the contrary—to suppose that the subject has the power to require performance or forbearance from the sovereign—implies another power superior to both subject and sovereign, by which the right was granted and which is capable of redressing the wrong resulting from its violation. If this other power exists, the ostensible sovereign is not really so, and a revolution has taken place or is in the act of taking place.

It is sometimes the fashion of truisms to promote fallacies. No better example can be found than in the comments of Burgess on the "principles which are termed laws of God, laws of nature, laws of reason and laws between nations." "It is conceivable," he says, "that an individual may, upon some point or other, or at some time or other, interpret these principles more truly than does the state, but it is not at all probable, *and not at all admissible in principle*. . . . Of course the state may abuse its unlimited power over the individual, *but this is never to be presumed*. It is the human organ least likely to do wrong, and, therefore, *we must hold to the principle that the state can do no wrong.*"

These statements are subject to almost every sort of objection. There is no occasion to invoke probabilities and presumptions when we are in possession of the facts. The truth is never inadmissible, and if politics is a science at all, it is surely not inadmissible to record one of the plainest facts of history—that upon a thousand points and at a thousand times individuals and groups of individuals have interpreted the principles of morality more truly than their sovereign. The further argument that because the state is the human organ least likely to do wrong, we must hold to the principle that it can do no wrong is even more indefensible. It is clear that when Burgess asserts that the state is the organ least likely to do wrong, he is referring to moral wrong. The correctness of this premise is open to doubt, but if we are persuaded to accept it we are told that we must conclude that the state can do no wrong. Unless the sentence presents a complete *non sequitur*, the meaning must be that there is a principle that the state can do no moral wrong. There is no such principle in either law or politics.

The importance of distinguishing between moral and political rights and wrongs can scarcely be overstated. We may not, however, dismiss the subject merely by noting that the distinction exists and that confusion is certain to result from the use of a single word to express two different ideas. As in the case of *duty*, the obligation, and *duty*, the tax, but in a plainer sense, the source of the difficulty lies deeper than any question of words.

No single sentence in Blackstone's Commentaries has been more frequently criticized than his definition of municipal law as "a rule of civil conduct prescribed by the supreme power in a state, *commanding what is right and prohibiting what is wrong*." The definition is bad because it is not true—the law issues many commands and prohibitions in which no moral principle is involved, and sometimes commands what is wrong and prohibits what is right. Blackstone goes on to say that when the boundaries of right and wrong are once established by law, it is the business of the law "to enforce *these rights*, and to restrain or redress *these wrongs*." We may pause to notice the delusive ease by which the moral rights and wrongs of the definition itself are converted into the political rights and wrongs that the law is to enforce or restrain. Now it is certain that in the definition Blackstone was using the adjective *right* in its ordinary and proper sense as a synonym of just or righteous, because he was paraphrasing a passage in Cicero, repeated by Bracton, and the Latin words are "jubens *honesta* et prohibens *contraria*." In Latin the word for *a right*, either legal or moral, is *jus*, so that Cicero could not have been misled by a verbal ambiguity. Nevertheless he fell into the very error that Blackstone has perpetuated.

The reason is clear enough. The law does not always command what is right and prohibit what is wrong, but there is a deep-seated and persistent human conviction that it ought to do so.

We shall encounter this conception again in a more literate and philosophic form under the name of natural law. At the moment it is enough to note that if it is bad morals to make power the test of righteousness, it is bad politics to make righteousness the test of legality. The first is the monstrous and inhuman error of Thrasymachus, which rejects all faith in a moral universe by asserting that justice is whatever the sovereign commands. The second is, if I may so express it, the sentimental error of Cicero and Blackstone, which rejects all experience by declaring that the sovereign always commands what is just.

We may now return to King Creon and his rebellious subject. Two propositions are plain. (1) She has no legal right against him and he can be guilty of no legal wrong to her. (2) Both of them have moral rights, though his are not in jeopardy, and both of them are subject to moral obligations. With these propositions in mind, let us proceed to give judgment.

What shall we say to Creon?

There is really no difficulty about the matter. With rare exceptions both political writers and moralists are in agreement that the sovereign is bound in conscience in the same way and to the same extent as the meanest of his subjects. Among political writers some of the supposed exceptions to the rule are apparent rather than real. Hobbes, for example, is often mentioned as if he might be quoted in defense of Creon, but the charge must be dismissed. "They that have Soveraigne power," he declared, cannot commit "Injustice or Injury in the proper signification"; but "it is true that they . . . may commit Iniquity." In decreeing that the body of Polynices shall be eaten by dogs Creon has committed iniquity, and we need have no hesitation in giving judgment against him.

What shall we say to Antigone?

We shall do well to recognize at the outset that it is possible to condemn her without falling into the heresy of Thrasymachus. Moralists as disinterested as Kant and churchmen as zealous as Gregory the Great have taught that kings are responsible to God alone and should be obeyed regardless of whether their conduct is just and lawful. Support for these contentions has been sought in the instructions of St. Paul to his Christian followers that "the powers that be are ordained of God," and that they who resist the powers resist the ordinance of God and "shall receive to themselves damnation." This is strong language, but it was certainly not intended as an argument to show that morality does not exist. On the contrary, it was intended as the expression of a moral precept, though it is worth noticing that if the precept were universally followed, the behavior of the political subject as such would be the same as if morality did not exist. Caesar might continue to order the killing of Christians, and Hitler the killing of Jews, and in either case the unconditional duty of the subject would be to obey.

But there is another point of view from which Antigone may be said to deserve vindication rather than censure. She does not regard the subject's duty of obedience as unconditional, and she is not alone in holding this opinion. According to Aristotle, political societies exist for the sake of noble actions. The end of the state is the good life—"an honorable and happy life." States are to be judged by their promotion of the welfare of all their subjects, and it is only in the perfect state that "the virtue of the good man is necessarily the same as the virtue of the citizen."

This point of view has never been entirely lost sight of in the political philosophy of the western world. In the Middle Ages it was as generally accepted by the apologists for the Emperor as by the apologists for the Pope. Among the former was the poet Dante, who wrote his *De Monarchia* to maintain the independence of the Empire against the claims of the pro-papal Guelfs.

The ideal monarch, he said, "will have all men good, which cannot be if they live under perverted constitutions: wherefore the Philosopher in his Politics saith, *That in a perverted Commonwealth the good man is a bad citizen; but in a rightful one* good man *and* good citizen *are convertible terms.* And the aim of such rightful Commonwealths is liberty, to wit that men may live for their own sake. For citizens are not for the sake of the Consuls, nor a nation for the King; but contrariwise the Consuls are for the sake of the citizens, the King for the sake of the nation. For as a Commonwealth is not subordinate to laws, but laws to the Commonwealth; so men who live according to law are not for the service of the lawgiver, but he for theirs; which is the Philosopher's opinion in that which he hath left us concerning the present matter. Hence it is plain also that though a Consul or King in regard of means be the lords of others, yet in regard of the end they are the servants of others: and most of all the Monarch, who without doubt is to be deemed the servant of all."

The occurrence of a situation in which one can no longer be both a good man and a good subject compels a decision one way or the other. Aquinas, buttressing his argument, as was his custom, by the authority of the patristic fathers, quoted with approval the saying of St. Augustine that "a law that is not just seems to be no law at all," and declared that human laws contrary to the commandments of God "should not be obeyed." In the philosophy of Azo of Bologna, a contemporary of St. Thomas, imperial edicts, if repugnant to natural justice, are "void." John of Salisbury (died 1180) recognized the "divine right" of rulers, but contended that it was subordinated to the divine law of a rational God. Suarez, the Jesuit, taught that there is a natural right to do what natural law bids, even against positive enactment, and that positive law, even if declared by the Pope, contrary to natural justice is a nullity. The undetermined Huguenot author of *Vindiciae contra tyrannos* held that if a tyrant breaks what the conscience approves as the law of God and true religion, there is a moral duty, not mere permission, to resist.

The implications of Aristotle's doctrine were written into our own Declaration of Independence. An unalienable right is a moral right that *ought to be made* a political right as well—a *claim* that ought to be supported by a *power*. The signers of the Declaration recorded their convictions that "to secure these rights, governments are instituted among men," and that "whenever any form of government becomes destructive of these ends, *it is the right of the people to alter or abolish it.*"

(The form of this statement comes from Locke and I consider it unfortunate. Revolution is never a political right. To admit as much is not, however, to deny that under certain circumstances it may become a moral duty.)

Our fathers built the politics of the Constitution on the morals of the Declaration of Independence. One of the avowed purposes of the new union was "to establish justice." When the Fugitive Slave Act was passed, the usually serene Emerson wrote in his diary: "I will not obey it, by God"; and his contemporary, William Lloyd Garrison, believing that justice could never be established so long as slavery persisted, denounced the Constitution as a "covenant with death and agreement with hell." In the more temperate language of philosophy it was the opinion of Emerson and Garrison that the virtue of the good man and the virtue of the citizen had ceased to be the same.

Unless we Americans have forgotten our revolutionary tradition, we cannot accept the proposition that, as a matter of morals, every command of the sovereign ought to be obeyed. In order to do so we should have to disown nearly all the great heroes in English history and in our own history. We should have to stand with King John against the barons at Runnymede, with James I against Coke, with the magistrates against William Penn, with George III against Washington, and with the sheriff against the fugitive slave. We should even have to forsake our legendary heroes, and make common cause with the Sheriff of Nottingham in hunting down Robin Hood and his merry men.

That good men are sometimes rebels and traitors is, indeed, much less a matter of philosophy than a matter of fact. On the whole it seems to me one of the characteristic and hopeful facts in the annals of Anglo-Saxon civilization in both the old and the new world. Moreover, whether as philosophy or fact, it is in every way less dangerous than its opposite. The record of peoples who have committed their consciences to the keeping of their sovereign—who have worshipped, like idolaters, the brazen leviathan of their own creation—is a record of sterility at home and ruthless aggression abroad. It is the record of Sparta in ancient times and of Germany, Japan, and Russia in our own time. Sovereigns are just like trees: by their fruits you shall know them. A state that brings forth good fruit is a good state and ought to be preserved. A state that brings forth evil fruit is an evil state and ought to be destroyed.

What, then, shall we say to Antigone? First of all, I think we must caution her. As even Jefferson recognized, rebellions are not to be justified by "light and transient causes." We must remind her that there are foolish martyrs as well as wise martyrs, and that when man acts as a political animal he is not absolved from the obligation of adopting a course that represents a judicious mixture of the cardinal and connected virtues of prudence and fortitude. (Professor Agassiz is reported to have said that the population of a German village would rise if two cents were added to the price of a glass of beer. Doubtless the price of a glass of beer is an insufficient reason for a political rising, but the world has witnessed the appalling consequences of the failure of the descendants of the very men of whom Agassiz spoke to regard any reason as sufficient for rising.)

But if Antigone is sure that she is right—if she is fully

persuaded that her cause is just and neither light nor transient—I think we must approve her violation of the edict and advise her to persist in it though the end is death. In the field of politics no philosopher can say more than that subjects must obey the commands of the sovereign or rebel against them. In the field of morals no casuist ought to say less than that God is greater than Caesar and that when Caesar commands iniquity, the duty of his subjects is to disobey. The importance of the latter statement is enhanced rather than diminished by the necessary admission that if the consciences of Caesar's subjects are wrongly informed, the good life is a dream that is incapable of realization. In politics, as in every other episode in the adventure of life, the price of moral freedom is the responsibility of acting at one's peril.

3. SOVEREIGNTY AND LIBERTY

That man is free who, subject to the laws,
Finds in his heart their origin and cause.

SOVEREIGNTY AND LIBERTY

"When love with unconfined wings
Hovers within my gates,
And my divine Althea brings
To whisper at the grates;
When I lie tangled in her hair
And fettered to her eye,
The birds that wanton in the air
Know no such *liberty* . . . . .

"Stone walls do not a prison make,
Nor iron bars a cage;
Minds innocent and quiet take
That for an hermitage;
If I have freedom in my love,
And in my soul am free,
Angels alone, that soar above,
Enjoy such *liberty*."

"The creature itself also shall
be delivered from the bondage
of corruption into the glorious
liberty of the children of God."

"I know not what course
others may take; but as
for me, give me *liberty*
or give me death."

"No person shall . . . be
deprived of life, *liberty*,
or property, without due process
of law."

IN THESE famous passages several ideas of liberty are presented. Lovelace, addressing Althea from prison, contrasts the liberty of the birds in the air with that of a lover who, though physically confined, is free in his soul, and affirms that the condition of such a prisoner is preferable to that of the birds and comparable only to that of the angels. St. Paul, addressing the Romans—and writing, if not actually from prison, at least in the shadow of prison walls—bears witness to the glorious liberty to be enjoyed by the children of God after their deliverance from the bondage of sin. Patrick Henry, addressing his fellow subjects of Virginia more than a year before the signing of the Declaration of Independence, proclaims by anticipation the watchword of the American Revolution. Three of our four authors have thus been identified. It remains to identify the fourth. In the bill of rights of the Constitution of the United States we read that no person shall be deprived of liberty without due process of law. Whose words are these and to whom are they addressed?

The Constitution mentions one kind of liberty and in so doing creates another. The liberty mentioned is not indeed exactly the same as that of the birds but in at least one obvious sense is more nearly related to it than to the imaginative and spiritual liberties extolled by the poet and the saint—for political purposes stone walls do make a prison and iron bars a cage. We are assured that this kind of liberty—"natural liberty" as it used to be called— will not be taken away without due process of law. By this assurance civil liberty, the liberty of politics, is established. We need not investigate the meaning of due process beyond an understanding of the fact that some sort of hearing is implied. The question is *by* whom the requirement of due process is imposed and *on* whom it is imposed. Since the essential characteristic of the political sovereign is the power to confiscate and condemn without a hearing, it is manifest that the constitutional prohibition is not directed *to* the sovereign of the United States. On the contrary, it is declared *by* the sovereign of the United States and it is directed *to* the federal government. (By the Fourteenth Amendment an identical prohibition was directed to the governments of the various commonwealths.)

We may take it for granted that nothing was further from the mind of Defoe than to write a political allegory in Robinson Crusoe. Nevertheless, one of the reflections that he has ascribed to his hero may be read with profit by every student of politics. "My island was now peopled, and I thought myself very rich in subjects; and it was a merry reflection, which I frequently made, how like a king I looked. First of all, the whole country was my own mere property, so that I had an undoubted right of dominion. Secondly, my people were perfectly subjected; I was absolutely lord and law giver; they all owed their lives to me, and were ready to lay down their lives, if there had been occasion for it, for me. It was remarkable, too, I had but three subjects, and they were of three different religions: my man Friday was a Protestant, his father was a Pagan and a cannibal, and the Spaniard was a Papist. However, I allowed liberty of conscience throughout my dominion. But this is by the way."

It may be by the way so far as the plot of Robinson Crusoe is concerned but it is directly along the way of our present inquiry. The language used is completely accurate except that Crusoe did more than to allow liberty of conscience to his subjects; in fact he created it for his subjects. Before he had made known his will their liberty, whether little or much, was only a condition like that of the birds—fortuitous and transitory—or, at the most, since human actors were involved, a moral right. The declared will of the sovereign superimposed a political right on a moral one and in so doing implemented a claim with a power. In politics, as in physics, power comes only from power.

A second characteristic of the right conferred by the Constitution is concealed rather than revealed in the narrowly restricted society of Crusoe's island. Many political rights, and among them those most commonly exercised, are granted *by* the government and are effective *against* individuals. If you are threatened with the loss of your property by robbery, you may call on the nearest policeman for protection. If you are a licensed physician, you may practice your profession without interference by private persons or even by unauthorized agents of the government. The constitutional provision does not purport to establish any right of this kind. The government

⟨ 38 ⟩

is not telling citizens how they are to behave toward
one another. Instead, the sovereign is telling the government how it is to behave toward citizens. No statute,
for instance, however regularly enacted, can deprive
the man arrested for robbery of the power to require
the officers in charge of the prosecution against him
to conform to whatever pattern may have been desig-
nated by the sovereign for the trial of accused persons.
It is the aggregate only of rights of this latter sort that
constitutes the field of civil liberty. Politically speaking,
all liberties are rights but only those rights that originate
with the sovereign and are effective against the government are liberties.

Let us suppose the case of a man who has been kid-
napped and held for ransom by private persons. So
long as stone walls make a prison, it cannot be denied
that the kidnappers have deprived their victim of his
liberty; but they have not deprived him of his civil liberty. What has happened is simply that the government
has failed in a particular instance to enforce the penal
code. No question of civil liberty—or, as we are accustomed to express such matters in the United States, no
constitutional question—is involved. For the same reason
no constitutional question is presented by the experience
of a speaker who is prevented from completing his speech
by the boos and catcalls of his audience. If I may so express it, the audience has as much right to boo as the
speaker has to continue—that is, neither one is the bene-
ficiary of a legal power to require forbearance from the
other. If a policeman is present in the hall in which the
disorder occurs, he may attempt to quiet the audience or,
if the disorder continues, he may escort the speaker from

the platform. In either event he acts only to prevent a
threatened breach of the peace. If, however, in the first
case supposed, the imprisonment had resulted from the
act of the government—or if, in the second case supposed, the policeman, without any threatened breach of
the peace, had prevented the speaker from continuing his
speech—a question would arise about the power of a subject to require forbearance from the government. In the
United States this question would be one of due process
under the federal bill of rights.

There is no need to multiply imaginary instances when
actual ones are at hand. One of the numerous decisions
involving the sectarians known as Jehovah's Witnesses
arose from the conduct of a member of the sect named
Cantwell, who had been engaged in selling religious tracts
and soliciting contributions on Cassius Street in the city
of New Haven. About ninety per cent of the residents
on this street were Catholics. Cantwell stopped two
pedestrians, both of whom turned out to be Catholics,
and requested their permission to play to them a phonograph record. They granted the permission and he
played the record. It contained a scurrilous attack on the
Catholic Church. Cantwell was arrested and convicted on
two charges—soliciting money for a religious cause without the certificate of authority required by a Connecticut
statute and conduct inciting others to commit a breach of
the peace. He appealed to the Supreme Court of the
United States, and the court set aside his conviction on
the grounds that the statute amounted to a denial of due
process by the Connecticut legislature, and that the play-
ing of the phonograph record did not create such a clear
and present danger of public disorder as to justify his ar-

rest by a Connecticut policeman and his conviction and sentence by a Connecticut court. I am not concerned at the moment with whether these determinations were correct as matters of constitutional law but only with the fact that Cantwell had a constitutional right to have his conviction reviewed. In the human issue between the parties our sympathies must go out to the angry pedestrians as the victims of a form of religious persecution that was not the less detestable because they were without a legal remedy to prevent it. Nevertheless, the persecution was of private origin, and as to them no question of civil liberty arose. On the other hand, Cantwell had been placed in jeopardy on one count by an act of the legislative branch of the government of Connecticut, and on another count by acts of the executive and judicial branches of the same government. In appealing he exercised the power to require forbearance that had been conferred upon him by the Fourteenth Amendment.

The nature of civil liberty is most clearly revealed in a state in which the limitations imposed by the sovereign on the government may be found within the four corners of a written constitution. For this reason most of the illustrations contained in this chapter have been drawn from cases arising or likely to arise under the Constitution of the United States. However, the conclusions arrived at are of universal applicability. They may be restated as follows. 1. Only the sovereign can create civil liberty. 2. Its field consists of the area of a circle described about the subject and within which the government is forbidden to act. Unless this circle has been described—by express declaration of the sovereign as in the United States or by constitutional usage universally understood and rigidly observed as in England—no civil liberty can be said to exist.

The tradition that bids us beware of the government suggests that we have more to fear from it than from either the sovereign or our fellow subjects.

So far as the acts of the sovereign are concerned, the question might be dismissed by saying that in any event the subject is without any sort of protection. If Pharaoh hardens his heart, his subject must submit or rebel. Nevertheless, while historical instances of the inconsiderate sovereign are by no means lacking, I think an argument could be made to show that there have been a hundred Hamans for every Pharaoh. It is not the great king but his wicked ministers; it is not the all powerful aristocracy but its corrupt and avaricious collector of taxes; it is not the sovereign people but their faithless agents and representatives by whom the good life has been most frequently imperiled.

So far as the acts of private persons are concerned, the great prohibitions of the penal code are everywhere declaratory not merely of commonly accepted theories of morality but also of the customary behavior of a vast majority of the population. Most people do not violate the law because they do not wish to violate it. The activities of the criminal minority are curbed, if not entirely prevented, by the government, and in consequence it has been true for hundreds of years that the average law-abiding subject in every civilized country can go to bed at night without having much reason to fear that his neighbors will burn his house about his ears. But there has never been a time when the average law-abiding subject *in every civilized country* could go to bed at night without having reason to fear a visit from the secret police. The man who says that he is willing to run that risk provided he is protected from the hazards of unemployment has never had any experience with the secret police.

The English and American conception of civil liberty is nearly or altogether unique in the history of political thought. A generation ago the English-speaking peoples were shaken by Homeric laughter at an incident that occurred in Imperial Germany known as the Kupenick robbery. An engaging rascal, who had served as a soldier and learned the drill and the passwords, came somehow into possession of the uniform of a captain, ordered the first company of soldiers he met to follow him, and, with the soldiers at his back, appeared at the town hall of a provincial town of some importance and demanded of the mayor the keys of the treasury. He got the keys without arousing any suspicion, robbed the treasury, and escaped with the money; and the robbery was not discovered until the accounts of the town were sent for approval to Berlin.

Given the necessary element of luck that the German impostor enjoyed, a like incident might happen now at many places in the world; but, of course, nothing at all resembling it could possibly happen in England or the United States. No English or American mayor would be impressed in the least by the uniform of a captain or any other military officer, however exalted in rank, or would be in any danger of forgetting that there is a power that protects citizens against the government and one branch of the government against encroachments by another branch. The President of the United States cannot give orders to the mayor of a city. A General of the Armies cannot give orders to a village policeman; and if the policeman makes an arrest without proper authority, the person arrested can sue him for damages in the ordinary civil courts.

A final question remains. The men of our race have been accustomed to reckon civil liberty as one of the greatest of human blessings. Is this appraisal correct?

Two answers to the question may be made. From the objective point of view, civil liberty is a blessing only if the political right on which the liberty depends is morally righteous. The power said to have been conferred in former times on the subjects of barbarous princes to pillage the property of shipwrecked aliens was a bad liberty because it served a bad purpose. The right more recently possessed by citizens of the United States to hold slaves as property without interference from the federal government was granted by a sovereign whose conscience had been wrongly advised, and in the end proved to be a curse rather than a blessing, and as much a curse for the masters as for the slaves.

From the subjective point of view, civil liberty is a blessing only if sovereign and subjects agree in general terms about what constitutes the good life. If the power to hold slaves is an example of a bad liberty, the power to require the government to refrain from quartering soldiers in private houses is an example of a dead liberty. Apart from moral considerations, the right of a convinced monogamist in a Mohammedan state to have a plurality of wives would be a dead liberty. Every liberty must be dead unless the power granted by the sovereign is in relief of a need that the subject has experienced.

Just here we come to a clue that leads from the liberty of the Constitution to the liberty to which, in the mind of Patrick Henry, there was no acceptable alternative but death, and to the "glorious liberty" of St. Paul's epistle. The historical movement in which Patrick Henry played so conspicuous a part began as a protest against what the American colonists regarded as unconstitutional acts by the British government—began, in short, as an attempt to secure an enlarged civil liberty from the British crown. It ended as a struggle for national independence by subjects who had become convinced that their sovereign neither understood them nor cared to understand them and that whatever liberty might be accorded to them would be alien and barren. The liberty of the "children of God" is glorious because they will to obey a law that finds its verification in their own hearts. If it were otherwise, there would be no meaning in the saying that man is made in the image of God. It is only when fundamental unity within the state is achieved— it is only when sovereign and subjects are made in the same image—that human liberty partakes, however imperfectly, of the glory concerning which the apostle has testified.

4. OF THE KINDS OF STATES

One rules, or few, or many. By this test
Three kinds of states are rendered manifest.

OF THE KINDS OF STATES

"Just as no good Brahman begins any literary work without a formula of salutation to Ganesa, the elephant-headed patron god of learning, so we in the West, though less punctilious about forms, might with some fitness open our undertakings in philosophy and science by saluting expressly or tacitly the memory of Aristotle." This advice is peculiarly appropriate here not only because Aristotle is universally and justly recognized as the father of the science of politics but also because the familiar division of states on the basis of the possession of sovereign power by the one, the few, or the many is commonly attributed to him. As a matter of fact the division did not originate with him, but it is nonetheless true that his contribution to the subject is greater than that of anyone else. Before discussing his views, it may be well to say a word about the nature of classifications in general.

A classification, as we cannot remind ourselves too often, is simply a device to aid us in thinking clearly—it is a servant, never a master. Therefore the merits of a proposed classification in any field of thought must be judged by its utility and accuracy under ordinary circumstances and in ordinary cases rather than by the readiness and certainty with which it will dispose of every conceivable or actually existing case. The distinction between the animal and vegetable kingdoms is a natural and useful one and is not to be discredited by showing that there are certain forms of life that cannot be assigned with confidence to either kingdom as against the other. Doubtless God does not think of life as divided into the animal and vegetable creations but it is convenient for men to do so. Moreover, classifications may be made for a variety of purposes, sometimes even for a frivolous purpose—

"Distinguishing those that have feathers, and bite,
From those that have whiskers, and scratch"—

so that it cannot be said that any one classification is universally right and all others wrong. You may, if you please, describe the Athens of Pericles as an ancient state or a European state as well as a state in which sovereignty was exercised by the whole body of citizens. The first description is concerned with time and the second with geography. If the last is for most purposes more significant than either of the others, the reason lies in the fact that sovereignty is the only essential characteristic of a state.

The poet has told us that when Homer smote his lyre he had heard men sing by land and sea and that among them were fishermen, shepherds, and sailors. In like manner I think we may assume that when Aristotle set about the composition of his *Politics* he was familiar with much that had already been spoken and written on the subject not only by Plato and other political philosophers but also by poets, historians, and citizens in the market place. Perhaps the earliest existing source of his triple classification is to be found in the second Pythian ode of Pindar (about 500 B.C.):

> "Yet in each state the candid man will go far,
> when *tyrants* rule, or the swirling *rabble*,
> or the *wise* keep the city in ward."

At all events the three forms were well known to Herodotus (about 450 B.C.), who recounts the debate about their relative merits among the conspirators who killed Smerdis, the usurper of the Persian throne, in 521 B.C. I quote the passage at length on account of its intrinsic interest and in order to show how little change has occurred in the nature of political arguments in the course of more than two thousand years.

"When the tumult was abated, and five days had passed, the rebels against the Magians held a council on the whole state of affairs, at which words were uttered which to some Greeks seem incredible; but there is no doubt that they were spoken. Otanes was for giving the government to the whole body of the Persian people. 'I hold,' he said, 'that we must make an end of monarchy; there is no pleasure or advantage in it. You have seen to what lengths went the insolence of Cambyses, and you have borne your share of the insolence of the Magian. What right order is there to be found in monarchy, when the ruler can do what he will, nor be held to account for it? Give this power to the best man on earth, and it would stir him to unwonted thoughts. The advantage which he holds breeds insolence, and nature makes all men jealous. This double cause is the root of all evil in him; sated with power he will do many reckless deeds, some from insolence, some from jealousy. For whereas an absolute ruler, as having all that heart can desire, should rightly be jealous of no man, yet it is contrariwise with him in his dealing with his countrymen; he is jealous of the safety of the good, and glad of the safety of the evil; and no man is so ready to believe calumny. Of all men he is the most inconsistent; accord him but just honour, and he is displeased that you make him not your first care; make him such, and he damns you for a flatterer. But I have yet worse to say of him than that; he turns the laws of the land upside down, he rapes women, he puts high and low to death. But the virtue of a multitude's rule lies first in its excellent name, which signifies equality before the law; and secondly, in that it does none of the things that a monarch does. All offices are assigned by lot, and the holders are accountable for what they do therein; and the general assembly arbitrates on all counsels. Therefore I declare my opinion, that we make an end of monarchy and increase the power of the multitude, seeing that all good lies in the many.'

"Such was the judgment of Otanes: but Megabyzus' counsel was to make a ruling oligarchy. 'I agree,' said he, 'to all that Otanes says against the rule of one; but when he bids you give the power to the multitude, his judgment falls short of the best. Nothing is more foolish and violent than a useless mob; to save ourselves from the insolence of a despot by changing it for the insolence of the unbridled commonalty—that were unbearable indeed. Whatever the despot does, he does with knowledge; but the people have not even that; how can they have knowledge, who have neither learnt nor for themselves seen what is best, but ever rush headlong and drive blindly onward, like a river in spate? Let those stand for democracy who wish ill to Persia; but let us choose a company of the best men and invest these with the power. For we ourselves shall be of that company; and where we have the best men, there 'tis like that we shall have the best counsels.'

"Such was the judgment of Megabyzus. Darius was the third to declare his opinion. 'Methinks,' said he, 'Megabyzus speaks rightly concerning democracy, but not so concerning obligarchy. For the choice lying between these three, and each of them, democracy, oligarchy and monarchy being supposed to be the best of its kind, I hold that monarchy is by far the most excellent. Nothing can be found better than the rule of the one best man; his judgment being like to himself, he will govern the multitude with perfect wisdom, and best conceal plans made for the defeat of enemies. But in an oligarchy, the desire of many to do the state good service ofttimes engenders bitter enmity among them; for each one wishing to be chief of all and to make his counsels prevail, violent enmity is the outcome, enmity brings faction and faction bloodshed; and the end of bloodshed is monarchy; whereby it is shown that this fashion of government is the best. Again, the rule of the commonalty must of necessity engender evil-mindedness; and when evil-mindedness in public matters is engendered, bad men are not divided by enmity but united by close friendship; for they that would do evil to the commonwealth conspire together to do it. This continues till someone rises to champion the people's cause and makes an end of such evil-doing. He therefore becomes the people's idol, and being their idol is made their monarch; so his case also proves that monarchy is the best government. But (to conclude the whole matter in one word) tell me, whence and by whose gift came our freedom—from the commonalty or an oligarchy or a single ruler? I hold therefore, that as the rule of one man gave us freedom, so that rule we should preserve; and, moreover, that we should not repeal the good laws of our fathers; that were ill done.' "

Doubtless Aristotle listened to similar arguments from the lips of his contemporaries. In adopting the three-fold division he added a subdivision that has not found general favor with later political writers. "The supreme authority in states must be in the hands of one, or of a few, or of the many"—but each of these forms is subject to a perversion which occurs when the power of the sovereign is used contrary to the common interest. The normal forms are monarchy, aristocracy, and πολιτεία—a word unhappily translated by Jowett as "constitution." The abnormal or perverted forms are tyranny, oligarchy, and democracy. "*Tyranny* is still always used in a bad sense, and *oligarchy* generally; but as to *democracy* Aristotle's distinction has fallen out of political language, perhaps because his term for the normal state was not specific enough. In English there would be no difficulty in using *commonwealth* or *republic* in Aristotle's good sense, and *democracy* in his bad one; but it has never been done." To attempt it now would serve only to make a confusing change in an almost universally accepted terminology.

A more important point is that Aristotle was perhaps writing about governments rather than states or, as seems to me more likely, did not clearly distinguish the state from the government. If so, the reason is doubtless the one mentioned in an earlier chapter: the distinction was not obvious in the small city-states of Greece, and Aristotle knew nothing at first hand about larger political societies. Indeed, it seemed to him that Babylon was too large to be considered a state at all because, as the story went, it "had been taken for three days before some part of the inhabitants became aware of the fact." One wonders what he would have had to say about modern states like the United States and Russia.

Now governments, as distinguished from states, have many characteristics, and no one of them may be adjudged to be of primary importance for all purposes or even for most purposes. According to one authority governments are (1) *immediate* or *representative*, depending on the identity or non-identity of the sovereign with the government; (2) *centralized* or *dual*, depending on the consolidation or distribution of governmental power; (3) *hereditary* or *elective*, depending on the tenure of persons holding office or mandate; and (4) *presidential* or *parliamentary*, depending on the relation of the legislature to the executive. Both immediate and representative government may be either (a) *monarchic*, (b) *aristocratic*, (c) *democratic*, or (d) may be a mixture of the three. Dual government is either (a) *confederate* or (b) *federal*; and so on. I do not mean to subscribe to this classification as a piece of political doctrine. I mean only to show that just as a horse may be accurately and usefully described as a quadruped from one point of view, a vertebrate from another, and a mammal from a third, so governments may be classified, with equal accuracy and utility, in a variety of ways according to the qualities considered and the ends intended to be served.

Subject to the qualifications already stated—about the nature of classifications in general and about the particular nomenclature that Aristotle employed—I am ready to accept his division *as applied to states* and to describe as a monarchy a state in which sovereign power is held by one person; as an aristocracy a state in which sovereign power is held by a few persons; and as a democracy a state in which sovereign power is held by the many. Let us not forget that we are discussing politics rather than economics. Capitalism, socialism, and communism are not theories of politics and have no necessary connection with any form of state. A monarchic state may have a socialistic economic structure just as it may have a democratic government. A democratic state may have a communistic economic structure just as it may have an aristocratic government.

My reasons for accepting the Aristotelian division are chiefly three. 1. It depends on what I regard as the only essential attribute of a state. 2. It is exhaustive, at least upon a proper definition of "few" and "many." (We have seen that England has a mixed form of government but there can be no such thing as a mixed form of state.) 3. It has been widely used both in philosophic writings and in common discourse for more than two thousand years and hence enjoys the enormous advantage of familiarity. Most of the difficulties arising from it may, I think, be resolved by careful consideration. If others prove to be insoluble, a failure or defect must be acknowledged; but I have already made it clear that I shall not regard that fact as an adequate reason, without more, for rejecting the classification as a whole.

What are we to understand by "few" and "many"? An immediate comment is that whatever we mean must be relative and indefinite, since the words themselves are not susceptible of accurate definition, or indeed of any definition except by reference to one another. In all the dictionaries that I have consulted the first definition given for "few" is "not many," though the corresponding definition of "many" as "more than a few" seems not to have been adopted by the lexicographers. According to the terminology preferred by Austin, if the sovereign group is small, the state should be called an oligarchy; if the group is of considerable size, an aristocracy; and if very numerous, a democracy. A serious objection to this division is that the word oligarchy is still commonly used in its Aristotelian sense to describe a bad or perverted aristocracy rather than a small one ("aristocracy misliked," as Hobbes expressed it). Moreover, as a great jurist has pointed out, "no one denies that there is a difference between night and day" and "the fixing of a point when day ends is made inevitable by the admission of that difference." We may attempt to avoid the troublesome fixing of the point by saying that there is a third something, neither night nor day, that can only be described as twilight. The attempt fails, however, since instead of one doubtful point there are now two—a point when day ends and twilight begins and a second point when twilight ends and night begins. In the same way, whatever difficulty may be encountered in the effort to distinguish between the few and the many is doubled instead of being removed by the necessity of determining the points at which a sovereign group ceases to be small and becomes of considerable size, or ceases to be of considerable size and becomes very numerous.

Does many mean most? In the opinion of Bodin and some later writers, an aristocracy exists wherever a smaller body of the citizens exercises sovereign power over the greater. This definition appeared to Hallam "to lead to consequences hardly compatible with the common use of language." He added that the electors of the House of Commons in England were not a majority of the people and inquired whether, on that account, they were to be regarded as an aristocratical body. In ancient Athens—which is generally reckoned as a democracy, though metics, slaves, and women were excluded from citizenship—not one-tenth of the inhabitants ever took part at any one time in the exercise of sovereign or governmental power. It is true that in those modern states, such as England and the United States, in which slavery has been abolished and universal suffrage prevails, the electors now are a majority of the people. Nevertheless, I think we must reject Bodin's rule of thumb as more likely to raise doubts than to settle them. It is better to run the risk of occasional uncertainty—it is better that a rare political specimen should remain unclassified—than to commit ourselves to the rigidity of a formula that would require us to deny the name democracy not only to the Athens of Pericles and the England of Hallam but also to the United States at all times prior to the adoption, in the year 1920, of the constitutional amendment conferring the franchise on women.

This brings us to a more substantial problem. It is

manifest that in at least one respect a democracy differs more widely from a monarchy or an aristocracy than either of these political forms differs from the other. In a monarchy or an aristocracy the one or the few are sovereign and the many are subjects; but in a democracy every voter is both a subject and a member of the sovereign group, and in states where the suffrage has been universally extended the electorate and the people have become so far synonymous terms that it is impossible to conceive a situation in which one decision is favored by the electors and another by the people. Thus democracy, which always presented itself as an approximation of self-sovereignty, has achieved in the modern world an identity between sovereign and subjects that is as nearly complete as the facts will allow.

We are accustomed to speak of the sovereignty of the people or of "the whole body of the people"—a form of words used by Marshall in his opinion in *Cohens* v. *Virginia* and echoed, no doubt unconsciously, by Professor Godley in translating the passage from Aristotle quoted above. Do such expressions correspond, even in a rough and general way, with political realities? An individual sovereign, at least if he is sane, can "make up his mind"—an enlightening phrase—about every question presented for his determination, and the members of an aristocracy, particularly a small one, may be and frequently are unanimous on all important issues. Can the mind of a people be made up in like manner from the discordant preferences and inclinations of the many individuals concerned?

The preamble of the Constitution of the United States is in the first person plural. In what sense, if at all, is it true that the people of the United States have set up a government and ordained and established a constitution? Having regard to the hard facts of politics, is there such a thing as popular sovereignty? Is the popular will at best a mere figure of speech and at worst a catchword of designing demagogues, or is it a real will that may be determined with at least a working degree of accuracy from time to time? The answers to these questions are of the first importance not only because of their bearing on the nature of democracy but also because of their relation to the conclusions at which we have already arrived about the nature of liberty.

5. POPULAR SOVEREIGNTY

Popular rule, as history discloses,
Depends on unity, not counting noses.

POPULAR SOVEREIGNTY

From one point of view, popular sovereignty is the re-animated ghost of Rousseau's theory of the general will. From another point of view, it is a metaphor for the rule of the majority or, at the strictest, for the rule of a plurality of the voting electors. I do not agree with Rousseau's theory, but neither do I believe that the sole or even the chief meaning of democracy is summed up in the convention of majority rule.

A certain mystical quality in the *Social Contract* no doubt accounts in part for the enormous influence that the book has exerted. There is a sense, not wholly irrelevant even in political discussion, in which democracy is always conceptual and approximate—becoming rather than being—and in which the perfect democracy will never be realized until the last man comes in. The statements made by Rousseau go far beyond an expression of this feeling. The sovereign, he declared, is always the general will, which is never "exterminated or corrupted" but is "always right," "always constant, unalterable, and pure." The sovereign is a collective being and, as such, can only be represented by himself. Hence the general will cannot be exercised except through the assembly of a whole people. Moreover, it may sometimes be so overpowered by particular interests as to find no expression even in such an assembly. There is a difference between the general will and the will of all—the former looks only to the common interest, whereas the latter is merely a sum of the wills of individuals. If it happened that a prince had "a particular will more active than the will of the sovereign, and should employ the public force in his hands in obedience to this particular will, there would be, so to speak, two sovereigns, one rightful and the other actual, the social union would evaporate instantly and the body politic would be dissolved."

Let us agree at once that all this is in the teeth of any workable theory of politics. In the first place, we have no reason to suppose that the general will (if there is one) is always constant, unalterable, and pure. The will of a monarch may be—and, as a matter of historical fact, often has been—more enlightened than that of his subjects. There is much force in the observation of Aristotle that "the many, of whom each individual is but an ordinary person, when they meet together may very likely be better than the few good, if regarded not individually but collectively, just as a feast to which many contribute is better than a dinner provided out of a single purse"—but to make this statement is only to assert a loose presumption that will probably be true in most cases or in the long run. In the next place, to say that the sovereign is always the general will makes it necessary to describe a prince who exercises absolute power as only a *de facto* sovereign. If this description is correct, the only *de jure* sovereign in Europe at the time Rousseau wrote his book was to be found in Switzerland

—everywhere else the body politic had been dissolved. But the real mischief is in the distinction itself. There is no such thing as a sovereign *de jure*—every sovereign is one *de facto* or not at all. Who ought to have absolute power is no more a political question than who is supposed to have it—the only political question is who actually does have it. Finally, there is additional mischief in the attempt to differentiate between the general will and the will of all, and in the conception of a popular sovereign as a "collective being" or, as other writers have expressed it, an "organism." I disagree strongly with every organic theory of the state. That the members of all political societies agree on some points, and that the members of some political societies are in substantially complete agreement on all important points, seem to me obvious truths which I shall have occasion to emphasize a little later on; but I can still find in these unanimities nothing beyond a significant identity in the wishes and opinions of the several individuals concerned. We are on the old road to political idolatry when we profess to have discovered, even in a democratic state, the existence of anything except the persons who compose it.

But in the account between posterity and Rousseau there are substantial items to be entered to his credit. Among them is the fact that he was one of the earliest political writers to distinguish clearly between the sovereign and the government or magistracy, which he defined as "an intermediate body set up between the subjects and the sovereign . . . charged with the execution of the laws." The *government* may be democratic, aristocratic, or monarchic; but the *sovereign* (or at least his sovereign *de jure*) is always the whole body of the people and therefore democratic. The government is simply the mechanism by which the general will is brought to bear on individuals or against other states, serving the same purpose in the state as the union of soul and body in the individual. In theory at least, this ideal is most likely to be realized where the government is democratic, because in that case the general will and the determinations of the government must necessarily coincide. But whatever the form of the government may be, frequent assemblies of the whole people ought to be held, in each of which two questions ought to be submitted in the first instance—(1) whether it pleases the sovereign to continue the present form of government and (2) whether it pleases the sovereign to leave the administration of the government in the hands of those at present charged with it.

We have already dismissed as contrary to fact Rousseau's contention that sovereignty always resides in the whole body of the people. While it is correct, as was conceded in an earlier chapter, that the existence of every government depends on what has been called the "generalized consent" of the people, the most superficial consideration will show that in certain states the government is, to a greater or less degree, effectively controlled by popular action, and that in others the "generalized consent" upon which the continuance of the political status quo depends is a mere acquiescence that may be motivated by anything ranging from apathy to terror. To maintain that in both cases the sovereign is still the whole body of the people is to confuse actual or presently potential power with power so vague and residual that its possession certainly does not constitute the sovereignty of practical politics.

But if it is not true that the general will always exists, is always sovereign, and is invariably constant, unalterable, and pure, it does not follow that the general will never exists or that, if it does exist, it is never sovereign. It does not follow, in short, that it is impossible for a state to be so constituted that supreme and irresistible power is actually exercised by the whole body of a people substantially of one mind about the kind of government to be established, the nature of the activities in which it is to engage, and the limitations to be placed upon it. This idea, which is largely ignored by the majority-rule democrats of the present day, is, I think, the really important contribution made to political philosophy by Rousseau.

I have more than once attempted to make a list of the fundamental convictions that are reflected in the political structure of the United States, and I find the enumeration both instructive and impressive. Among them are that a democratic government is better than either a monarchic or an aristocratic one; that a system of private property is to be preferred to communism; that the judiciary should be independent of both the executive and the legislature; that church and government should be completely separated; that a candidate for public office should not be disqualified because of his religious views; that monogamy is the most desirable form of the marriage relation; that trial by jury is an essential safeguard of civil liberty; and that freedom of speech and of the press ought to be protected from governmental interference.

Most of these convictions (and the list might readily be expanded) are expressed, in whole or in part, in the Constitution of the United States, and, from long familiarity, seem to us like truisms. But they are not truisms. The merits of democratic government have never been universally admitted throughout the civilized world. The Russians do not share our view about private property; nor the English about an established church and an independent judiciary; nor the Irish about religious tests; nor the Arabs about polygamy; nor the people of continental Europe generally about trial by jury and freedom of speech and of the press. The Constitution of the United States is not a restatement of the undebatable postulates of politics. It is rather a summary of the elements that most Americans agree in regarding as essential to the enjoyment of the good life.

It has been considered anomalous that Austin and his followers, along with American political writers, have been "driven to assign the title of sovereign to an authority which may be active not more than once or twice in a century, or else to confound sovereignty with the ultimate and unformed political control of the people at large." I think we may escape both horns of this dilemma. If the only measure of activity is change, it is correct that the sovereign of the United States was active only four times during the nineteenth century—i.e., in the exercise of the amending power. By the same test a housewife is never active except when she is moving the furniture about. But there is another sense in which at least the first of the two questions proposed by Rousseau —whether the existing form of government shall be continued—received daily consideration from the sovereign and was answered in the affirmative with only four exceptions in the course of a hundred years. In so saying we are not confounding the sovereign with the *Zeitgeist*. We are simply giving due recognition to the fact that the electorate affords a broad target on which the shafts of the *Zeitgeist* may fall.

Because complete unanimity is never attained, the claims of minorities are sometimes ignored or overruled. No better illustration can be found than the case of the Mormons. Here is a church whose members believed (and some of whose members probably still believe) that the practice of polygamy is morally and socially meritorious or at least unobjectionable. If a large majority of their fellow citizens agreed with them, the bill of rights of the Federal Constitution would contain a clause prohibiting both Congress and the legislatures of the commonwealths from interfering with polygamy, or its practice would have been protected by the Supreme Court as a "liberty" under the existing language of the due process clause. As matters actually stand, no protection has been afforded or is likely to be afforded—and this without regard to the sincerity with which the convictions of the Mormons may be entertained. The result meets with the approval of the overwhelming majority of our people, but as to the Mormons themselves we must recognize that the compulsion to which they are subjected is in no way different from a like compulsion suffered at the hands of a sovereign individual or minority. It is as true in a democracy as anywhere else that where there is no will to obey there can be no liberty in obedience.

But there is an unwritten unanimity which has not been

mentioned and which is the source of an essential mechanism of the democratic process, though a mechanism of relatively narrow range. Sir Henry Maine has noted that the practice of taking the opinion of the majority as the opinion of the entire group is so familiar to us that it seems natural, although in fact "nothing can be more artificial." "Where," asks Rousseau, "unless the election were unanimous, would be the obligation on the minority to submit to the choice of the majority?" His answer is that "the law of majority voting is itself something established by convention, and presupposes unanimity, *on one occasion at least.*" The answer is correct—our unwritten unanimity is that matters not regarded as of fundamental importance may be determined by an election and that we will be bound by the decision of a majority of the voters. We are not willing to submit to this convention the questions of whether our lives are to be forfeited or our right of free speech is to be denied, but we are willing to submit to it the determination of who is to be President of the United States, because we are all persuaded that the election of any of the candidates is desirable from one point of view and at least tolerable from every other. With less caution, the inhabitants of some of the ancient democracies were content to have matters of this latter sort settled by lot.

Professor Santayana has summed up the matter in what seems to me one of the wisest of political comments.

"The practice of English liberty [in the United States]," he says, "presupposes two things: that all concerned are fundamentally unanimous, and that each has a plastic nature, which he is willing to modify. If fundamental unanimity is lacking and all are not making in

the same general direction, there can be no honest co-
operation, no satisfying compromise. Every concession,
under such circumstances, would be a temporary one, to
be retracted at the first favourable moment; it would
amount to a mutilation of one's essential nature, a partial
surrender of life, liberty, and happiness, tolerable for a
time, perhaps, as the lesser of two evils, but involving
a perpetual sullen opposition and hatred. To put things
to a vote, and to accept unreservedly the decision of the
majority, are points essential to the English system; but
they would be absurd if fundamental agreement were
not presupposed. Every decision that the majority could
conceivably arrive at must leave it still possible for the
minority to live and prosper, even if not exactly in the
way they wished. Were this not the case, a decision by
vote would be as alien a fatality to any minority as the
decree of a foreign tyrant, and at every election the right
of rebellion would come into play. In a hearty and sound
democracy all questions at issue must be minor matters;
fundamentals must have been silently agreed upon and
taken for granted when the democracy arose. To leave
a decision to the majority is like leaving it to chance—a
fatal procedure unless one is willing to have it either way.
You must be able to risk losing the toss; and if you do
you will acquiesce all the more readily in the result, because, unless the winners cheated at the game, they had
no more influence on it than yourself—namely none, or
very little. You acquiesce in democracy on the same conditions and for the same reasons, and perhaps a little more
cheerfully, because there is an infinitesimally better
chance of winning on the average; but even then the
enormity of the risk involved would be intolerable if

anything of vital importance was at stake. It is therefore actually required that juries, whose decisions may really be of moment, should be unanimous; and parliaments and elections are never more satisfactory than when a wave of national feeling runs through them and there is no longer any minority nor any need of voting."

The practical limits to the practice of settling questions by vote have often been shown. The framers of our Constitution, for example, wrote into it a provision that no religious test should ever be required as a qualification to any office or public trust under the United States. The article in question expresses a widely held opinion that the religious views of public officials are not matters of vital political importance. Doubtless a large body of citizens voted against Alfred E. Smith for President because he was a Catholic, but there is surely no experienced observer who believes that if he had been elected a rebellion would have occurred. In Ireland, however, where the memory of old wrongs makes it as unbearable for Catholics to be governed by Protestants as for Protestants to be governed by Catholics,—and also in India, where an even greater degree of bitterness prevails between Moslems and Hindus,—a decision by vote becomes, as Santayana says, "an alien fatality" by which it is known in advance that the minority will refuse to be bound. The difference has nothing to do with intelligence or political capacity. It results rather from the almost universal prevalence in the United States of an attitude toward religious issues that is not equally prevalent in all parts of the world. As a mere matter of definition, we may not assert that if the whole of Ireland or of India were presently organized into a political society in which the many were sovereign, the result would not be a democracy. But we may maintain with confidence that if such a state were established, it would prove to be unstable and that a condition of anarchy would be certain to arise.

This conclusion requires the addition of a final item to our list of unanimities. The proposition that only matters of minor importance may be settled satisfactorily by the convention of majority rule implies as its converse that matters of major importance may be disposed of only by a consensus of opinion among members of the sovereign group—that is, by a degree of working agreement approximating the ideal of complete agreement toward which democracy continually reaches but never entirely achieves. The existence of this self-denying unanimity is recognized in most written constitutions, including the Constitution of the United States, by provisions intended to prevent the exercise of the amending power at the instance of a simple majority of the voters. This device is, at the best, an awkward one. It is even more artificial than majority rule, and a good deal has been and may be urged against it—e.g., that the only alternative to majority rule is minority rule and that, as Hamilton pointed out, "to give a minority a negative upon the majority (which is always the case where more than a majority is requisite to a decision), is, in its tendency, to subject the sense of the greater number to that of the lesser." We must acknowledge the force of this criticism, though it is a curious fact that most of the modern writers who advance it do not seem to realize that a plurality of the voting electors is usually not only less than a majority of the people but also less than a majority of the electorate, so that in nearly every instance their "majority rule" is also minority rule. At all events these critics lose sight of the reason underlying the constitutional requirement: in a "hearty and sound democracy" every citizen must be assumed to feel for the fundamental law as a whole a loyalty deeper than he can feel for any specific measure by which it would be so changed as to become obnoxious to a large minority of citizens.

This sentiment is a commonplace in the ordinary affairs of life. A man may belong to a voluntary organization such as a lodge or bar association. At a meeting of the organization a resolution may be offered to which, by way of first impression, the member feels that he will give his support. In the ensuing debate it may become apparent that the resolution is probably favored by a majority of those present but that if it is passed a minority of the membership will be bitterly aggrieved. Under these circumstances, the member, without changing his original opinion, may and often does vote against the resolution on the ground that the advantages to be gained from its passage are less than the disadvantages of a disagreement so deeply felt as to menace the very life of the organization.

The wisdom of every such decision depends, of course, on the facts of the actual case in which the necessity for deciding occurs. In the decades immediately preceding the American Civil War there were patriotic men both north and south of Mason and Dixon's Line who believed that the solution of the question of slavery in a particular way was more important than the preservation of the Union. In a famous letter Abraham Lincoln dissented from this opinion. If it is argued that, as the event showed, the majority was strong enough to compel both the abolition of slavery and the maintenance of the Union, the answer is that no majority can permanently hold in subjection a resolute and uncompromising minority, and that the Union has been preserved only because of the ultimate acceptance by almost every American of the view that Lincoln expressed. Our history has been a fortunate one. To the extent that it has been exceptional it should not blind us to the truths that voting is not a democratic principle but a democratic method, and that unless the majority, either in obedience to a constitutional requirement or by voluntary self-restraint, is willing to tolerate the continuance of a way of life regarded by the minority as essential to the pursuit of happiness, no democracy can long endure.

6. GOVERNMENT AND POSITIVE LAW

Who seeks the sources of the law must see
Things as they are, not as they ought to be.

6

GOVERNMENT AND POSITIVE LAW

THE word law has even more meanings than the word liberty. Among a great variety of other things, it is used to describe (1) an observed sequence in the order of natural phenomena—e.g., the law of gravity, (2) an observed sequence in the behavior of human beings—e.g., Gresham's law, (3) the principles governing righteous conduct—the moral law, (4) the expression of right reason, inhering in nature and man, and having ethically a binding force as a rule of civil conduct—the natural law, (5) the rules of a game—e.g., the laws of whist, (6) the rules of a church or other voluntary organization—e.g., the canon law, (7) a body of precepts adopted by treaty or convention but without any means of enforcement— e.g., international law, (8) the sentence or decree of a prince or potentate—e.g., the law of the Medes and the Persians, (9) the usages followed by the members of a particular trade or profession—e.g., the law merchant, (10) a traditional system of practice and procedure—e.g., the law of the land, (11) a constitution, (12) the order of an administrative body, (13) the decision of a judge or magistrate, and (14) a statute adopted by a legislative body. In what follows I am referring only to that sort

⟨ 79 ⟩

of law with which the science of jurisprudence is concerned, "law in the lawyer's sense," as it has been called —an apt and informal phrase, which certainly includes some of the illustrations given above and equally certainly excludes others.

Even in this restricted sense the nature and sources of the law is a subject that has given a vast deal of trouble to legal scholars. I agree with Gray that "the great gain . . . which jurisprudence made during the last century was the recognition of the truth that the law . . . is not an ideal, but something which actually exists." It is not "the art of what is good and equitable," as Celsus said; or "that which reason in such sort defines to be good that it must be done," as Hooker said; or "the abstract expression of the general will existing in and for itself," as Hegel said; or "the organic whole of the external conditions of the intellectual life," as Krause said. *It is something.* What is it?

1. According to Austin and his followers, law consists of the commands of the sovereign. "Every Positive Law," he says, "obtaining in any community, is a creature of the Sovereign or State: having been established immediately by the monarch or supreme body, as exercising legislative or judicial functions: or having been established immediately by a subject individual or body, as exercising rights or powers of direct or judicial legislation, which the monarch or supreme body has expressly or tacitly conferred."

There is a sense in which this is true, of course, but it is a highly artificial sense. Haman was no doubt the creature of Ahasuerus, but it is not easy to understand how an order given by Haman without the knowledge or even in violation of the wishes of his master can be said to have been the "creature" of the master—conceding for the sake of argument that any command can be said to be a creature at all. Maine has put the case at its strongest in a striking passage about Runjeet Singh, the chieftain of the Sikhs, who seemed at first sight to be a complete embodiment of Austin's conception of sovereignty. "He was absolutely despotic. Except occasionally on his wild frontier, he kept the most perfect order. He could have commanded anything; the smallest disobedience to his commands would have been followed by death or mutilation, and this was perfectly well known to the enormous majority of his subjects. Yet I doubt whether once in all his life he issued a command which Austin would call a law. He took, as his revenue, a prodigious share of the produce of the soil. He harried villages which recalcitrated at his exactions, and he executed great numbers of men. He levied great armies; he had all material of power, and exercised it in various ways. But he never made a law." Nevertheless, as Maine goes on to point out, laws were continuously administered throughout his dominions by domestic tribunals. Difficulties of this sort drove Austin into his famous dictum that "whatever the Sovereign permits he commands." Here also I agree with Gray: "it is certainly a forced expression to say that one commands things to be done, because he has the power (which he does not exercise) to forbid their being done."

The fact is that no sovereign is familiar with all of the law to which his subjects conform or, under modern conditions, with any considerable part of it; and the further fact is that no sovereign greatly cares what some of the law is. It would be a mistake to suppose, however, that he does not care what any of it is. The sovereign people of the United States have shown no interest up to the present time in the divorce laws of any of the commonwealths; but they have insisted upon the maintenance everywhere of the concept of due process, and—to take an example whose notoriety proves its exceptional character—they were once so much concerned about the marriage laws of Utah as to have required the insertion in its constitution of an article forbidding polygamy and providing that the prohibition is irrevocable except by consent of the United States. Generally speaking, the importance of sovereignty in the field of jurisprudence appears to me to have been unduly stressed. The sovereign makes liberty, and in the course of doing so makes constitutions (and therefore law of a sort, chiefly of a negative sort); but for the great body of the law we must find some other origin.

. 2. According to a second theory, the law lives in the common consciousness of the people and, as the matter is sometimes expressed, the duty of the judges is simply to "discover" it. "The foundation of the Law," says Savigny, "has its existence, its reality, in the common consciousness of the people. This existence is invisible. How can we become acquainted with it? We become acquainted with it as it manifests itself in external acts, as it appears in practice, manners, and custom: by the uniformity of a continuous and continuing mode of action, we recognize that the belief of the people is its common root, and not mere chance. Thus, custom is the sign of positive law, not its foundation." In order to deal with an obvious objection, he is compelled to add that when the law becomes so developed in its details that it can no longer be mastered by the people generally, a separate class of legal experts is formed which, itself an element of the people, represents the community in this domain of thought, and that henceforward the law leads a double life. "In its fundamental principles it continues to live in the common consciousness of the people; the exact determination and the application to details is the special calling of the class of jurisconsults."

It is one of the curiosities of the history of legal thought that Savigny, who was a German, expressed a point of view that is characteristically English, whereas Austin, whose definition of law as the command of the sovereign is typically Germanic in spirit, was an Englishman. In the time of Savigny, as well as before and afterwards, the jurisconsults endeavored almost without exception to compel an acceptance of the principles of Roman law without regard to, and often directly against, the wishes of the German people. On the other hand, the language of Savigny has been a commonplace time out of mind on the lips of English judges, who were denounced by Austin for perpetuating "the childish fiction . . . that judiciary or common law is not made by them, but is a miraculous something made by nobody, existing, I suppose, from eternity, and merely *declared* from time to time by the judges."

I think the real error in Savigny's doctrine is not that it involves a fiction but that it confuses the law that is with what, from his point of view, must be regarded as the law that ought to be, and hence would deny the term not only to the rules of conduct imposed upon a subjected population but also to all rules that are at

〈 83 〉

variance with the common consciousness of the people. The behavior of the inhabitants of India was regulated for centuries with little regard to their own beliefs and practices. Must we affirm, then, that in the true sense there was no law in India during the whole of that period? The Court of Star Chamber was a hated court in England, and the excise, if we are to believe Dr. Johnson, was "a hated tax." The Alien and Sedition Acts and the Fugitive Slave Act were equally hated by a majority of the people of the United States. Are we forced to conclude that the decrees of the Court of Star Chamber and the excise tax, however regularly issued or enacted, were never the law in England? Must we go beyond characterizing the Alien and Sedition Acts and the Fugitive Slave Act as bad laws and say that they were never laws at all? We may, of course, answer all these questions in the affirmative, but if we do so we are again, as in the case of Austin's definition, using words in a sense so unusual as to be positively misleading.

It is to be noticed that Savigny does not argue that custom *is* law. He argues that the law is rooted in the belief of the people and that custom is its "sign," not its foundation—a form of expression that calls to mind the words put by Kipling into the mouth of Sir Richard, the Norman, in praising his Saxon friend in *Puck of Pook's Hill*: "His Saxons would laugh and jest with Hugh, and Hugh with them, and—this was marvelous to me—if even the meanest of them said that such and such a thing was the Custom of the Manor, then straightway would Hugh and such old men of the Manor as might be near forsake everything else to debate the matter—I have seen them stop the mill with the corn half ground—and if the custom or usage were proven to be as it was said, why, that was the end of it, even though it were flat against Hugh, his wish and command."

"Now, my Lord," said Chief Justice Holt, speaking in "The Great Case of Monopolies" in this very tradition, "I do think, that practice and usage is a great evidence of the law." And there is authority for the statement that the idea of law as antecedent to any written or oral announcement of it was so deeply rooted not only in the minds of English judges but also in the spirit of the people themselves that it was not until the thirteenth century that Parliament abandoned the pretense of declaring what the common law was and ever had been, and began avowedly to make new laws by statute.

All this seems to me of enormous interest and importance, though it has more to contribute to an understanding of liberty than of law. Indeed, in the legal documents of early England "liberty" and "custom" were used almost as interchangeable terms. Thus in chapter 13 of Magna Carta the *"liberties and customs"* of London and other cities and seaports were confirmed, and chapter 39 of one of the first republications of the charter provided that no freeman should be "disseised of his freehold or his *liberties or his free customs* or be outlawed or exiled or otherwise destroyed but by lawful judgment of his peers, or by the law of the land." A custom is a practice—something that people *do*—and the best evidence of what people think is not what they say or, for that matter, how they vote, but how they habitually behave. As we have learned to our cost, when the citizens of a democratic state support prohibition at the polls but continue to drink alcoholic beverages in their daily lives, something has gone wrong with the recording mechanism. Other illustrations are easy to find. At many places throughout the United States the statutes and ordinances regulating the speed of motor vehicles have little relation to the practices and experience of persons commonly considered to be careful drivers. In a majority of jurisdictions the courts have laid it down that a man who fails to stop, look, and listen at a railroad crossing is guilty of negligence, on the ground that his conduct falls short of the standard of care that would be exercised by a reasonable man—whereas the fact is that not one reasonable man in a hundred thousand stops at every railroad crossing. If we accept Savigny's views, we may characterize these as bad laws which, at the best, can command only a grudging obedience. But if his theory were pushed to its limits, we should have to declare that they are not really laws at all; and with this pronouncement I have already indicated that I cannot agree.

Just here we must distinguish between the relationship of law and custom in a democracy and in any other form of state. Where the sovereign is other than democratic, there is no reason in logic why any such relationship should exist. Recurring for a moment to Agassiz's villagers, who would rise if two cents were added to the price of a glass of beer, the most we can say is that only an imprudent prince would order the increase likely to produce the rising. Nevertheless, if the offensive order were made, the only remedy, short of rebellion, available to the thirsty subjects would be to petition for a redress of grievances. But in a political society having both a democratic sovereign and a democratic government the law is supposed to express the popular will, and if it fails to do so the injured citizens may, and sometimes do, take the necessary steps to alter or abolish it. If the obnoxious law is of statutory origin, a new legislature may be chosen and the statute may be stricken from the books: in the case of the Alien and Sedition Acts, the offensive legislation was not only repealed but fines collected under the Sedition Act were repaid. If the trouble is one of judicial interpretation, a statute to meet the unpopular decision may be enacted or, if a constitutional question is involved, an appropriate amendment to the Constitution may be adopted: less than five years after the Supreme Court had determined that the judicial power of the United States extended to a suit brought against a commonwealth by a citizen of another commonwealth, the court was instructed by the blunt phraseology of the Eleventh Amendment that the Constitution should "not be construed" in that way. Finally, if the will of the sovereign has been misstated or has undergone a change, as in the case of the Eighteenth Amendment, the declaration that was never authentic or that has ceased to be authentic may be repealed. I think Savigny's doctrine applies only (and even then not universally) to what law *ought to be* in any state and is *supposed to be* in a democracy. It may even apply to what law *actually is* in an extremely simple political society like that of England before the Norman conquest. But it certainly will not serve as the basis for a general definition.

3. A third theory declares that "the law of a community consists of the general rules which are followed by its judicial department in establishing legal rights and

duties" or, in somewhat different language, it is the rules which the courts *will follow* in establishing these rights and duties. For many years one of the burning questions in the field of jurisprudence was whether there is such a thing as judge-made law. Pollock has called attention to a passage in the Year Books in which an English judge of the fourteenth century asserted (Sir Frederick thought in jest) that the law was "what the Justices will," and was rebuked by his brother in the words, "No; Law is reason." If we are compelled to choose between these definitions, the first is certainly to be preferred. If the law is reason, everything that is not reason is not law—a proposition so palpably absurd that no refutation is required. Conceding, however, that courts make law—conceding, that is to say, that the original issue has been resolved in favor of the affirmative—is it true that the law is what the judges will *and nothing else?* Is it true, in short, as some of the modern realists would have it, that everything except the rules laid down by the courts must be regarded as sources of the law rather than as the law itself?

Under the statute formerly in force in the commonwealth in which I live, the widow of a man dying without issue and without leaving a will became entitled to half his estate, instead of the entire estate as in many other jurisdictions. Quite recently the statute was changed so as to include the latter provision. The amendment operated only prospectively, and in the regular course of events could not be applied by the courts for a period of weeks or months after its effective date. In the meantime, however, lawyers had informed their clients of the action of the legislature, wills had been made and other instruments had been drawn with the altered language in mind, and for certain purposes it was presumed that the content of the amending act had been brought to the attention of every citizen. How shall we describe what occurred? Are we to say that the sovereign, having permitted a change in the intestate laws of a particular commonwealth, must be understood as having commanded that the change be made? Are we to say that the common consciousness of the people of that commonwealth required this particular reform? Are we to say that what was reason on one day became unreason on the next? Are we to say that the act of the legislature furnished the legal profession with evidence justifying the prophecy that the law was *about to be changed?* Or shall we say, finally, that the law *was changed* by the amendment of the statute? This is what the lawyers told their clients, and I submit that any other form of words does violence to the realities of the legislative process.

The opponents of the theory that judges sometimes make law have been fighting a losing battle for more than a century. Doubtless the time has come when they must be brought to acknowledge that the battle is lost; but in dictating the terms of surrender it does not follow that we must include in them an article declaring that the courts are the only law makers. "I recognize without hesitation," said Holmes, "that judges do and must legislate, but they can do so only interstitially; they are confined from molar to molecular motions." This sounds so much like Osric that we may well inquire with Horatio whether it is "not possible to understand in another tongue." I think it is: if judges legislate only interstitially, they do not do all of the legislating; and if they are confined from molar to molecular motions, the confining force in the case of the interpretation of a statute is to be found in the language of the enactment that they are called upon to expound. If the President of the United States or the policeman on the corner is authorized by the legislature to exercise a particular discretion or to accomplish a particular result, he necessarily interprets in some degree the statute by which the authority is conferred. In so doing he does and must legislate. It is true that, on an appeal to the courts, his interpretation may be rejected or the statute may be declared unconstitutional. Hence in any contest between the legislative or executive and the judicial organs of the government, "it is the judicial which has the last say as to what is and what is not law in a community." But it is also true that this last say is usually just amen. Numberless statutory enactments receive an executive construction which is never challenged, or are so plainly worded that to all intents and purposes they require no construction; and the constitutionality of not one statute in a hundred is ever called into question.

I suggest that most of the difficulties encountered in this chapter will disappear if one point is kept in mind— with rare exceptions the law consists of a body of rules and determinations originating with the government. I am not attempting a new definition or even a complete description. I mean only that a particular key fits a good many of the locks with the opening of which the science of jurisprudence is concerned.

If the law is the "creature" of the government, we are released at the outset from the embarrassments of the maxim that the sovereign commands whatever he permits. "After all," as a modern writer puts it, "to say that the little law maker acts on behalf of the big law maker involves a needlessly metaphorical way of getting what we are after. All we need to say is that we conceive of the legal order as forming a sort of hierarchy in which those things happening on the lower levels derive their validity from the fact that they happen within the framework established by the higher levels of the order. . . . When the judge makes law he is not making it on behalf of anyone else; he is simply exercising a function allotted to him under an assumed constitutional order."

We are likewise released from the difficulties inherent in the metaphysical attempt of Savigny and his followers to identify the "big law maker" with the *Zeitgeist* and in the spurious realism that is able to recognize the "little law maker" only in the judicial branch of the government. If it is a forced expression to maintain that the sovereign is the only law maker because he has the power (which he does not exercise) to forbid what the statutes or the courts command, it is an equally forced expression to contend that the courts are the only law makers because the process of judicial construction, like the similiar one of executive construction, sometimes adds to or subtracts from the text that has been received from the ostensible legislator, or even because they have the power (which they seldom exercise) to set aside the work of the legislator on constitutional grounds. We may admit that, once the declaration of unconstitutionality has been made, the statute ceases to be the law; but to argue that it was never the law because in the end the courts refused to follow it is no less metaphysical than to assert that the Alien and Sedition Acts were never the law because the event showed that they did not have their existence in the common consciousness of the people of the United States.

William James said that the properties of a bit of blackboard chalk were whiteness, friability, cylindrical shape, insolubility in water, etc., etc., and that "if God should keep sending them to us in an unchanged order, miraculously annihilating at a certain moment the substance that supported them, we never could detect that moment, for our experiences themselves would be unaltered." Substance, says the philosopher, is revealed through its attributes, and if a given bit of matter has all the attributes of chalk, it is chalk so far at least as human purposes are concerned. The properties of the law are as well known to most of us as those of a bit of blackboard crayon. They are sent to us in one form or another by the President and the policeman, by the Supreme Court of the United States and the rural Justice of the Peace, by boards and commissions, by Congress and town councils, and by a score of other organs of general and local government. Without engaging in the philosophical issue between nominalists and realists, I think we must conclude that what looks, tastes, and smells like law, *is* law; and that, generally speaking, law making is part of the ordinary business of the government.

7. E PLURIBUS UNUM

A sovereign whole of sovereign parts? Beware!
Omnipotence is either here or there.

E PLURIBUS UNUM

WE AMERICANS ought to know more about the science
of politics than any people on the face of the earth. The
history of the United States is a pageant, marvelously
condensed and foreshortened, in which the answers to
nearly all the great political questions may be found. The
pageant began with a revolution. Not long after independence had been won, the system of government under
which we are living was established all at one time and
substantially in its present form. If an Englishman wishes
to understand the powers and limitations of his government, he must explore the precedents of almost a thousand years. We need do no more than to turn to the text
of a written instrument that was signed in Philadelphia
a little more than a hundred and fifty years ago. This
is a very short period of time if we measure by the grand
calendar of history. It is not a long one even if we
measure by the petty calendar of our own lives and those
of our immediate ancestors: I have eaten dinner with a
man who in his youth had eaten dinner with a man who
had seen George Washington and Benjamin Franklin
talking together on the steps of Independence Hall.

Our fathers caused the familiar words *e pluribus unum*

—from many one—to be inscribed on the great seal of the United States. Afterwards the course of events made it uncertain whether the inscription represented an aspiration, a prophecy, or the sign and record of an accomplished unity. An issue about the location of ultimate power which had been more or less apparent from the foundation of the government, and which proved to be so vital and insistent that it could neither be compromised nor ignored, gave rise to a civil war. The war was fought to a terrible and decisive conclusion. No people, ancient or modern, has been so deeply concerned as ourselves with the political problem of the one and the many or has paid so high a price to find out what the solution of the problem is.

We noticed in an earlier chapter that *governments*, as distinguished from *states*, may be classified in a variety of ways and for a variety of purposes, and that by one method of classification they may be described as *centralized* or *dual* depending on the consolidation or distribution of governmental powers. In England the government is centralized, in the United States dual. This does not mean that there is no local government in England. It means that the local government is statutory rather than constitutional in principle—i.e., there is no local government created by the sovereign, no local government that the general government cannot legally change or destroy. We noted in addition that dual government is either *confederate* or *federal*. Under the confederate system, there are a number of states coextensive as to territory and population with an equal number of local governments, and one general government. Under the federal system, there is one state coextensive as to territory and population with the general government, and a number of local governments.

Prior to the Revolutionary War thirteen English colonies had been established along the eastern seaboard of the North American continent. Each of these colonies had a separate government that had been created directly or indirectly by the sovereign of the English state. No problem of classification was presented. The political situation was as old as the fact of colonization itself: there were thirteen governments in America but no state.

Every schoolboy knows that in the year in which the former colonies achieved their independence, they entered into a "firm league of friendship" providing, among other things, for the maintenance of a general government. Whatever practical difficulties were inherent in this arrangement, the political situation was still too plain to be misunderstood. There were now thirteen states with fourteen governments—one in each of the states and the general government set up under the Articles of Confederation. The result was a confederacy (confederation, league, and alliance are other names for the same thing) and the Articles constituted a treaty or compact among the contracting parties. One of the conditions of the treaty was that no amendments might be made except by unanimous consent. Although the union was described as "perpetual," it was never believed by anyone that the use of this word implied a moral obligation on the part of the members not to secede, much less that their political power to secede had been limited or abridged. Moreover, the Articles themselves explicitly stated that each state retained "its sovereignty, freedom, and independence." A sovereign state *ought* to keep its promises perhaps, but it *can* break them or it is not a sovereign state.

Every schoolboy also knows that about six years after the ratification of the league of friendship, certain delegates of the states, who had been appointed "for the sole and express purpose of revising the Articles of Confederation," violated their instructions and undertook to set up a new general government in the name and by the authority of "the people of the United States."

Beard thought it significant that as late as seven days before the convention that framed the Constitution had finished its work, the Preamble of the draft read: "We the people of the States of New-Hampshire," etc. Since, however, the convention had adopted a resolution that, when ratified by nine states, the new constitution should go into effect as applied to those nine states, "leaving the other four out in the cold," the Committee of Style concluded that it would be a mistake to name all the states in the document, because some of them might decide to stay out of the Union. This, in his opinion, "is a case of men's building better than they knew—or of an incidental matter before the Committee of Style leading to one of the strangest and most momentous prophecies of all history." Before commenting on this statement, three points are to be considered: (1) what the delegates to the convention were authorized to do, (2) what they purported to do, and (3) what actually happened. The first two points present questions of law. The third presents a question of politics.

1. The answer to the first question has already been given—the delegates had been empowered to do no more than suggest improvements to the Articles of Con-

federation. The only *legal* course open to the convention was to prepare a preliminary draft or plan and submit it to Congress in the hope that that body would agree to it and recommend its adoption by the legislatures of all of the states.

2. The delegates adopted a radically different procedure. They inserted as the final article in the new constitution a provision that ratification by *conventions* called in nine of the thirteen states should be sufficient to establish the Constitution among the ratifying states. They then adopted a resolution transmitting the result of their labors to Congress and suggesting that it should be "submitted to a convention of delegates, chosen in each state *by the people thereof*, under the recommendation of its legislature, for their assent and ratification." It is interesting to notice that the reference to conventions chosen *by the people* appears in the resolution rather than in the text of the Constitution. In effect, the delegates, though clothing their proposals in moderate and legal language, were going over the heads of both Congress and the existing state legislatures and were appealing directly to the people for approval of the authority that they had assumed. As matters turned out, the article about the nine states proved to be unrealistic. For geographical reasons the new general government could not be put into operation without the adherence of New York, and no attempt to put it into operation was made until the Constitution had been ratified by the convention called in New York, which was the eleventh state to ratify.

3. The question of what actually happened is less easy to answer. When the Constitution had been ratified by

all the members of the old confederation and formal unanimity had thus been obtained, it was apparent that there were still fourteen governments—the old general government having been replaced by the new one—but doubts immediately arose as to whether there were thirteen states or only one: whether the United States remained as a league of states with a *confederate* government or had become a single state with a *federal* government; whether there were still a number of states coextensive as to territory and population with an equal number of local governments, and one general government—or one state coextensive as to territory and population with the general government, and a number of local governments. In the ensuing debates some men spoke of the Constitution as if it were a contract, and presented arguments based on the supposed intention of the contracting parties. Other men, unable or unwilling to face the crisis that impended, repeated the comforting rhetoric of Webster about a sovereign nation of many sovereign states. The event demonstrated that the warning of John Randolph that to ask a state "to surrender part of her sovereignty is like asking a lady to surrender part of her chastity" had been wise as well as witty. When the last gun of the Civil War had been fired, it was clear that there is a single collective sovereign in the United States, and therefore only a single state.

In spite of the clarity of the record, the nature of our institutions has not always been understood by European observers. Thus even so competent a critic as Pollock has laid it down in the course of an exposition of the modern theory of the state that "a statute of Rhode Island made in due form and within the powers reserved to State legislatures by the Constitution [of the United States] cannot be legally overruled by any human authority." While "it is true that the Constitution itself provides ways of amendment," the amending authority "has no power to legislate in detail for any State. It can add articles to the federal Constitution; it cannot enact a new statute for Rhode Island." Certainly no citizen of that commonwealth can read these statements without a sense of astonishment. On January 16, 1920, the Eighteenth Amendment prohibiting the manufacture, sale, or transportation of intoxicating liquors throughout the United States became effective. Rhode Island had expressly rejected the amendment. The statutes on her books authorizing and regulating the sale of intoxicating liquors had been "made in due form" and were clearly "within the powers [theretofore] reserved to state legislatures by the Constitution." Nevertheless, every one of them was "legally overruled." The people of the United States could (and did) "legislate in detail" for every commonwealth in the union. They could (and did) "enact a new statute for Rhode Island." They can (and will), unless and until they lose the power that they now possess, set up that sort of government which pleases them, and change it from time to time as their wishes may change.

If these propositions are correct, it must also be correct that a revolution occurred at some point in our history between the ratification of the Constitution and the end of the Civil War. I am not using the word revolution in its Jeffersonian sense of an overthrow of the government by the sovereign, but in the larger and (as I think) more accurate sense of a shift of sovereignty—the passing of supreme and irresistible power from the allied sovereigns who joined in the Articles of Confederation to the people of the United States in whose name the Constitution was ordained.

When did this shift of sovereignty take place? Many political writers insist that the delegates to the constitutional convention initiated a *coup d'état*, and that the revolution must be dated from the adoption of the Constitution. On this theory the Civil War may best be described by the name by which it was formerly known in the North—the War of the Rebellion. A reason sometimes advanced in support of the theory turns on the fact that the action of the convention, while seeming to leave the old government intact for non-assenting members of the Confederacy, actually destroyed it for all the members. The argument is that if the people of nine states supposedly (eleven actually, less than all in any event) could overthrow the government, supreme power must have been in their hands in the very hour when the Constitution was ratified. The conclusion may be sound, but the reasoning is certainly faulty. The people of a *single state* could have ended the confederate government and the Confederacy itself at any time by secession, exactly as a single partner can terminate a partnership at any time by withdrawal. Moreover, if the seceding member had happened to be New York, the twelve remaining members would have been so situated geographically that it would have been impossible for them to form a new confederacy; but if this division had occurred, no one would contend that the act of the people of New York, however disruptive, was that of the sovereign of the United States.

This brings us to a second interpretation. By the

ratification of the Constitution eleven of the thirteen original sovereigns withdrew from the league of friendship and formed a new league, which was promptly joined by the other two sovereigns. The association continued to be of the confederate type, although the powers of the general government were considerably enlarged and those of the local governments correspondingly diminished. Almost three quarters of a century after the league had been established, some of the original states, along with other states that had been admitted to membership in the meantime, attempted to secede. The resulting struggle was not a rebellion. It was a War Between the States—the name by which it is commonly called in the South. The war ended in a popular revolution by which all of the warring states were destroyed and a new state with a federal government was born.

Under either interpretation I agree with Beard that the language of the preamble was a prophecy. Doubtless the date of its fulfillment cannot be accurately determined. Perhaps, indeed, we can do no better than to adopt the phrase attributed by Maine to Fitzjames Stephen and describe the period between the ratification of the Constitution and the beginning of the Civil War as one of "dormant anarchy"—a period, that is to say, in which the forces of a political society are in a state of temporary equilibrium and in which the members of the society, hoping vainly that life will prove less terrible than logic, strive to postpone or to avoid altogether the test by which in the end the seat of sovereignty must be determined. But I do not agree with Beard that the prophecy of the preamble was the result of "an incidental matter before the Committee of Style." After all, there is some connection between words and things and, as every lawyer knows, the careful drafting of a legal instrument often throws an unexpected and revealing light on the true relationship in which the parties to the instrument stand. The difficulty experienced by the committee did not lead to the momentous prophecy to which Beard has referred. It arose in the nature of the case because the prophecy was about to be made. In deciding to announce the creation of a new government the delegates to the convention acted in the teeth of their instructions and without even a semblance of legal authority. At some point in their deliberations they were bound to ask themselves for whom they were acting—i.e., what source of actual authority they claimed to represent. The embarrassment about style was only a symptom of a deeper and inescapable embarrassment about political realities.

All this may impress the reader as no more than a piece of barren speculation about

> "old, unhappy, far off things
> And battles long ago."

There is a sense in which this may be true; but in a larger and more imaginative sense the lesson to be learned from those things is one for our time and for all time. Nearly all the proposals that have been presented for the federation of the world are founded upon one or the other of two conflicting assumptions—that it is possible to form a state in which supreme and irresistible power is located in several places at once, or a state in which such power is nowhere to be found. The course of our history has impressively demonstrated that both assumptions are false.

In setting up a federal government in the United States our fathers enjoyed two advantages. The second was very nearly essential to the success of the experiment, and I shall refer to it a little later on. But the first was completely essential and I must state it at once. The thirteen sovereigns of the old confederation were all democratic. In each of these states the people were in control, and hence were in a position, if they saw fit to do so, to surrender their power and to join with the peoples of the other states in the formation of a new sovereign group.

We have been told, sometimes explicitly but more often by implication, that, in like manner, "we, the people of the earth," can and should ordain and establish an all inclusive constitution. However disastrous the consequences may be, the suggested analogy is wholly false. In most of the states now existing in the world the people are not in control. On the plainest grounds they cannot *give up* what they do not *have*. If they do not possess sovereign power now, they cannot yield it and, in the absence of a series of revolutions, they cannot unite with other peoples in seizing the power that their present rulers exercise and in organizing a democratic sovereign for the world. In the opinion of Kant, the problem of the establishment of a world republic, "hard as it may sound, is not insoluble even for a race of devils, if intelligent." He was mistaken. Intelligence is not enough. A race of either saints or devils can establish a world republic, but in order to do it they must be all-powerful as well as intelligent.

The second advantage possessed by our fathers was the existence among the people of the thirteen states of that substantial unanimity about fundamentals which has been mentioned in an earlier chapter as a necessary condition of the successful operation of a democratic political society. The inhabitants of the states occupied a contiguous territory, spoke a common language, and had inherited or acquired by experience a common cultural and political tradition. It is easy to see now that the apprehensions which made it doubtful whether the Constitution would be ratified arose in most instances from nothing more than unreasonable prejudice. The citizen of Rhode Island who thought that he could not trust the citizens of New York or Pennsylvania to vote about questions that concerned his dearest rights had no true reason for alarm. The conception of the good life was essentially the same in all of the states, and it was certain that the voters of New York and Pennsylvania would impose no burdens on themselves that would prove abhorrent to their neighbors.

Here again the suggested analogy breaks down. No similar like-mindedness prevails throughout the world today. I am not thinking chiefly about clashing economic philosophies. I am thinking rather about rights like free speech and a free press, which cut deeper than any theory of property.

That a majority of the people now living in the world set less store by these rights than ourselves seems to me to be self-evident. I do not mean to imply that our definition of the good life is in all respects superior to theirs. If we have much to teach, we have also much to learn. Perhaps we have more to learn than we have to teach. It may even be (though I do not believe it) that we value too highly rights of the sort to which I am referring. All these considerations are beside the point. Wisely or foolishly, perhaps as heroes and perhaps as bigots, our ancestors have loved liberty and have been willing to fight for it on two continents and for almost a thousand years. If the people actually exercised sovereign power in every state in the world, the situation would be vastly more encouraging than it is; but even if this were so, we could not join *now* in the creation of a universal state unless we were prepared to place in jeopardy at the outset the oldest and most deeply felt of all our political traditions.

Are we then forced to conclude that the parliament of man and the federation of the world are only poetical dreams like the Golden Age and that there will be no end to the international anarchy that has characterized western civilization since the fall of the Roman Empire? Eddington remarked that there was no obvious physical reason why, having once arrived, man should not continue to populate the earth for another ten billion years or so. Without abandoning historical time for any such astronomical figures, it is easy enough to catch with Holmes, "beyond the vision of battling races and an impoverished earth . . . a dreaming glimpse of peace."

I take it to be as certain as anything can be that unless the human race is about to destroy itself, a time is not far distant when a single state, whatever its form may be, will exercise dominion over the whole world, and will impose a *pax Romana* on those backward or dissenting peoples whose wishes run counter to those of the sovereign individual or group. Much later, thousands of years later, we may suppose that a time will come when there will no longer be any backward or dissenting peoples, when the same idea of the good life will be universally held, and the inhabitants of the earth will, like the reconciled partisans of Lancaster and York,

> "in mutual well-beseeming ranks
> March all one way."

Shall we pray for the hastening of that day? *The answer depends entirely on the direction of the march.* There are good dreams and bad dreams. The dream of Holmes was of a race "bred to greatness and splendor by science." As we should know well enough, science does not always breed men to either greatness or splendor. Perpetual peace might be the fulfillment of a beatific vision, but it might also be the reenactment of a nightmare. A time will never come when peace will be more important than righteousness.

8. DEMOCRACY AND NATURAL LAW

A blessing mitigates the primal curse
Of knowledge of the better and the worse—
Reason in man, as in the universe.

DEMOCRACY AND NATURAL LAW

TAKEN at its strongest, it is only in a theoretical sense that a universal case for democracy can be stated here and now. As we have seen, popular sovereignty is not a political device like the Australian ballot or proportional representation to be adopted or rejected at pleasure. It is a political fact that may be shown to exist in certain states and not to exist in others. Where the fact occurs, as, for instance, in modern England, the traditional reiteration in British statutes that the King is sovereign is no more effective to take from the people the power that they actually have than the recital in the statutes of the later Roman Empire that the people were sovereign was effective to restore to them the power that they had permitted to slip out of their hands. In the case of a conquered political society it is possible, of course, for the victors to set up a democratic *government*; but the moment the forces of occupation are withdrawn—the moment, that is to say, when the independence of the society is restored—the old question about the location of ultimate power is certain to recur. An ardent wish on the part of almost every inhabitant for the establishment of a democratic state will enhance the likelihood of resolving the question in the desired way, but it will not ensure a settlement in that way. A democracy is not born because people yearn for political power but because they seize it. Every revolution begins as an idea but it ends as a fact. Moreover, not every popular revolution begets a democratic state. If the revolutionists have nothing in common except hatred for a particular sovereign, they will abdicate their power as soon as the object of the revolution has been attained, and sovereignty will be assumed by a new individual or group. We are reminded of the uncharacteristic lines of Wordsworth about

"the simple plan
That they should take who have the power,
And they should keep who can."

Simple or not, the only plan by which democracy can become a working reality is for a people, at once like-minded and willing to make compromises, to take the power and keep it.

When this phenomenon presents itself, how are we to evaluate it? The pursuit of this inquiry involves more than the weighing and measuring of Leviathan. It requires a consideration of the distinctions between good and evil, right and wrong, and justice and injustice; the nature of human destiny; and the ways of God to man.

An attempt to justify democracy may be, and sometimes has been, made on what, by a sort of equivocation, may be described as pessimistic grounds. At its baldest the attempt comes to this. If I live in a state having a population of 100,000,000 people, I have only one chance in 100,000,000 of being sole sovereign and only one chance in a million of belonging to an aristocracy of a hundred. But if the state happens to be democratic, I have one chance in two of sharing the opinion of the majority on every public question and of being on the winning side at every election. (As Santayana points out, my own vote makes the chance "infinitesimally better" than one in two.) Moreover, I have a right to be heard, and if I am eloquent and pertinacious in argument, I may succeed in changing the minds of some of my fellow citizens who disagreed with me at the outset.

The argument to be drawn from Aristotle is less explicitly self-regarding but equally pessimistic. You will remember that he classified states on the basis of the possession of sovereign power by the one, the few, or the many and subdivided each class into its good and perverted forms. In their good forms the sovereignty of one is best and that of the many worst. However, in their perverted forms an inverse order occurs—the sovereignty of one is worst and that of the many best. Hence, since states are more often perverted than good, the rule of the many constitutes on the average the safest type of political organization.

A modern and different sort of pessimism finds its expression in the writings of Holmes. In his youth he had been accustomed to say that "truth was the majority vote of that nation that could lick all the others," and on reconsideration in after years thought that "the statement was correct in so far as it implied that our test of truth is a reference to either a present or an imagined future majority in favor of our view." Therefore it seemed to him the strongest argument against persecution for the expression of opinions that "when men have realized that time has upset many fighting faiths, they may come to believe even more than they believe the very foundations of their own conduct that the ultimate good desired is better reached by free trade in ideas—that the best test of truth is the power of the thought to get itself accepted in the competition of the market, and that truth is the only ground upon which their wishes safely can be carried out." Montesquieu had declared that the most perfect government is that which attains its ends with the least cost, so that the one which leads men in the way most according to their inclinations is best. "What," asked Holmes, "have two hundred years added? What proximate test of excellence can be found except correspondence to the actual equilibrium of force in the community—that is, conformity to the wishes of the dominant power? Of course, such conformity may lead to destruction, and it is desirable that the dominant power should be wise. But wise or not, the proximate test of a good government is that the dominant power has its way."

There is music here, but it is not the music to which our fathers marched. They professed "a decent respect to the opinions of mankind," but to suppose that the opinions of mankind furnished a definition or even an ultimate test of the truths to the defense of which they had pledged their lives and fortunes would have seemed to them an indecent disrespect to truth itself. They did not measure excellence in government by the closeness of its conformity to the wishes of the sovereign—they did not judge the fruits by the trees. Instead, they judged the trees by the fruits—the fitness of the sovereign to rule by the qualities of the government that he established. They thought it not impossible that they, as men of good will, should enlist the power of Leviathan in order to lay the earthly foundations of the City of God.

Let us compare Holmes's argument in favor of free speech with the one advanced by Gamaliel almost two thousand years earlier. Gamaliel was speaking about the members of a religious society who taught what seemed so revolutionary a doctrine that certain of their countrymen took counsel to slay them. His advice was this: "Refrain from these men and let them alone: for if this counsel or this work be of men, it will come to naught. But if it be of God, ye cannot overthrow it; lest haply ye be found even to fight against God." Both arguments enjoin tolerance, but the philosophies underlying them are as far apart as the poles. Gamaliel sought to convince his listeners that the truth is certain to prevail in the end; Holmes that whatever prevails in the end must be accepted as true whether we like it or not. I find it hard to believe that he acted on his own doctrine. I find it hard to believe that he was willing to die at Antietam for no better reason than the conviction that an imagined future majority, say, in the year 2000, would favor his view, or that victory for the cause in which he fought would bring about a political correspondence to the actual equilibrium of force in the community!

Our fathers thought of the state not as an organism but as a mechanism, whose aim was liberty—that "men may live for their own sake," as you will remember that Dante expressed it, or, as I have expressed it, that men may render willing obedience to a law that finds its authority and verification in their own hearts. Such men are free because they command themselves. The course of history has shown that, with rare and brief exceptions, all sovereignty except self-sovereignty is tyranny. It is not true that all power corrupts; but in the long run the only political power that does not corrupt is the power that a free people exercises over itself.

This conception of liberty is important only if persons are important. Forbidden foolishness is no more wisdom than forbidden wickedness is virtue, and to speak of enforced wisdom and enforced virtue involves a contradiction in terms; but the contradiction is of no practical significance unless certain assumptions are made. We must be concerned with the trees rather than with the forest. A tree is a thing, but a forest is only a collective noun used to describe a number of trees located in a particular place. "Mankind?" asked Goethe, and replied: "It is an abstraction. There are, always have been, and always will be, men and only men." Persons exist like trees; but society and the state are convenient mental classifications, not external realities.

If we reject this philosophy, it can make no difference whether the members of society behave in a specified way because they have chosen wisdom and virtue or because they have been coerced into obedience. But if we accept it, we must likewise accept "the Kantian injunction," against which Holmes "rebelled," that every human being must be regarded "as an end in himself and not as a means."

Must we conclude then that no price is too big to pay for liberty and that, where the necessary factual basis for democracy is present, it is better to follow the path of folly as free men than the path of wisdom under compulsion? If we agree, for the sake of argument, that tariffs are among the chief causes of war, is it better for a people strongly convinced of the merits of a tariff to court destruction than to be ruled by a monarch who would enforce free trade? Aristotle would have answered this question no—a wise monarch is the best ruler of all, but it must never be forgotten that such rulers are few and far between. Holmes would have answered the question yes—wise or not, the test of a good government is that the dominant power has its way. Jefferson, who spoke in what I regard as the authentic democratic tradition, would also have answered yes, though for a different reason—democrats must play high, and in the case supposed there is at least a justifying chance that the people will learn the advantages of free trade in time to secure peace without losing their liberty.

It is clear that we have come to a parting of the ways. If we are to defend democracy as our fathers conceived it, we must do more than deny that justice is only the interest of the stronger. We must affirm that the distinctions between good and evil and justice and injustice depend on objective reality, and that men are endowed with the capacity to draw these distinctions, though perhaps always imperfectly, and with freedom of will to choose between the alternatives presented—and we must add to these affirmations a special and optimistic article of faith: that where popular sovereignty and civil liberty exist, the people, even if at long last and at great cost in blood and treasure, will choose wisely and well. These are the classic postulates of democracy. The moral philosophy on which they depend is to be found in the teachings of Christianity. It is also to be found in the much older doctrine of natural law which, under one name or another, has been current in every civilized age.

While modern aberrations have led to a widespread belief that natural law is "only a cloak for arbitrary dogmas and fancies," its history shows that, far from exalting private judgment, it has never ceased to rest its claims on what is an essentially rationalist and progressive tradition. Five hundred years before the Christian era, Lao-tze taught his disciples that "only that government has value which is in accord with nature or the *Tao* (Reason)." The Stoics deduced natural law from the rational and divine order of the world; and Cicero, who followed the Stoic tradition, accepted it as the basis of his legal philosophy and declared that "the discipline of law is drawn from the innermost nature of man." Roman jurists like Gaius and Ulpian sometimes identified it with, and sometimes distinguished it from, what they called *jus gentium* or the law of nations—i.e., the common law or usage of mankind, not to be confounded with international law arising from treaty or compact. The English common law concepts of a reasonable man and a reasonable price are based upon it. Wherever the doctrine occurs and however it may be expressed, its proponents share the conviction of Aristotle that "there really is, as everyone to some extent divines, a natural justice . . . that is binding on all men"—a conviction that is repeated not only in Justinian's Code and in the daily pronouncements of our own equity judges, but also in the passionate though less literate insistence of the man in the street that "what's right is right" and that "there ought to be a law" to make this right a political reality.

Some writers, chiefly modern, will tell us at once that beliefs of this sort cannot be proved in the scientific sense and hence have no place in political discussion. We may admit the premise while dissenting from the conclusion. In order to make good the dissent we need not argue that politics must be regarded as a branch of ethics. We need only remind ourselves that moral considerations are completely relevant wherever human actors are involved. That this truth has been lost sight of too frequently in recent years has created a philosophic vacuum that has been quickly filled by the supporters of doctrines fraught with what seems to me a menace to civilization itself.

Let us take heart of comfort yet. None of the great questions that have commanded the attention of men since civilization began can be settled one way or another in the scientific sense. It is as true today as it was in the time of the great apostle that in the wisdom of God the world does not know God through wisdom.

Suppose it to be demonstrated, as I think it could be, that it is impossible to guarantee that a dictator who has seized supreme power will always use it to good effect, or, if he is sane and of good will today, that he will be so next year, or that his successor will be; that it is likewise impossible, once a dictator has taken supreme power, to remove him except by revolution; that it is likewise impossible for a dictator, even if sane and of good will, to consider personally the welfare of a hundred million subjects; and that, therefore, in the absence of free speech and a free press, it is impossible for him to instruct and control his agents so as to do justice. If this demonstration were made, the ordinary man would be fully convinced of the evils of a dictatorship, but the philosophical skeptic would not be convinced of anything.

"The law's our yardstick, and it measures well
Or well enough when there are yards to measure.
Measure a wave with it, measure a fire,
Cut sorrow up in inches, weigh content."

I cannot do it and nobody else can do it. We cannot measure and weigh sorrow and content because they are purely subjective; but what is more important for present purposes is that we cannot persuade the skeptic that *any* values are other than subjective. We cannot persuade him, for instance, that the doctrine of the dignity of man has any basis except emotion; or that it is better to liberate slaves than to enslave the free; or that kindness is to be preferred to cruelty. We may convince him perhaps that the many are more merciful than the one or the few, but we cannot convince him of the quality of mercy.

But if men are to think at all they must begin somewhere and, as Holmes himself recognized, pure skepticism cuts away the foundation on which all thinking stands. "We begin," he wrote to his Chinese correspondent, Mr. Wu, "with an act of faith." Apparently, however, a very small act of faith will suffice, since he was at pains to assure Mr. Wu that he had been quite serious in an earlier letter in asking how Wu knew that he was not dreaming Holmes. Perhaps he was thinking of the doubts of the Chinese philosopher: "Once upon a time, I, Chuang Tzu, dreamt I was a butterfly, fluttering hither and thither, to all intents and interests and purposes a butterfly. I was conscious of following my fancies as a butterfly, and was unconscious of my individuality as a man. Suddenly I awaked, and there I lay, myself again. Now I do not know whether I was then a man dreaming I was a butterfly, or whether I am now a butterfly dreaming I am a man."

We may repudiate doubts of this sort in our own philosophy even though we cannot refute them, and if we make the repudiation, we shall do so the more cheerfully, and not the less confidently, because all history shows that when large numbers of people align themselves with the disciples of Pyrrho rather than with those of Socrates and Aquinas—when they doubt whether they doubt, or whether the mind is an instrument capable of correct thinking, or whether they are men or butterflies—the barbarians are at the gates. If the doubters were wise, they would welcome the barbarians, if only for the zest to be gained from a reinvigorated certitude. There is, I believe, no instance of a healthy barbarian who was troubled by uncertainty about whether he was a man or a butterfly.

But if modern subjectivism entails the risk of inducing in philosophers less tough-minded than Holmes an abject and perverted humility, an opposite risk is also involved. We are not confronted here with the sophisticated query of Pilate. ("'What is truth?' said jesting Pilate, and would not stay for an answer." I do not agree with Bacon that he was jesting. I think he was skeptical and sad, and that he did not stay for an answer because he felt sure that no satisfactory answer could be made.) We are confronted rather with the menace of that "cosmic impiety" against which Bertrand Russell has sounded so impressive a warning. "The concept of 'truth' as something dependent upon facts largely outside human control has been one of the ways in which philosophy hitherto has inculcated the necessary element of humility. When this check upon pride is removed, a further step is taken on the road toward a certain kind of madness— the intoxication of power which invaded philosophy with Fichte, and to which modern men, whether philosophers or not, are prone. I am persuaded that this intoxication is the greatest danger of our time, and that any philosophy which, however unintentionally, contributes to it is increasing the danger of vast social disaster." If we adopt Peirce's definition of truth as "the opinion which is fated to be ultimately agreed to by all who investigate," the hazard, as Russell sees it, is not that we shall fall to the barbarians. The danger is rather that we shall *become* the barbarians, because, when we cease to believe that men can find the truth and come to believe that they can make it, we put it in the power of the sovereign to render any horror respectable by coercing the investigators into a spurious agreement. This is not the "ultimate" agreement that Peirce had in mind, but if we are to be guided by it in our daily lives, we must necessarily treat it as ultimate.

There are difficulties in any theory of natural law which must instantly be acknowledged. The political writers of the realistic school can never be too much commended for insisting that natural law is not "law in the lawyer's sense"—that the law that ought to be is seldom, perhaps never, precisely the law that is, and hence that it cannot be called law at all unless we clearly understand that we are using the same word in two different, though originally related, senses. Even the moderate statement of Pollock about the "principles of conduct . . . common to and admitted by all men who try to

behave reasonably" leaves some of the difficulties un-
solved. Doubtless a body of such principles may be for-
mulated, but a review of their application, even in their
most general terms, presents a record that is partly
equivocal and partly self-contradictory. I am not thinking about the opinions of a half-mad philosopher like
Nietzsche who rejected the principles themselves. I am
concerned rather with the views of great and sane thinkers
like Plato and Aristotle. That human slavery is an iniquitous institution is a proposition that would meet with
almost universal acceptance at the present time; yet both
Plato and Aristotle expressly justified slavery on moral
grounds by arguments which, so far as I know, were
unchallenged in what was perhaps the most enlightened
age in the history of mankind. Clearly, then, in order
to determine what natural justice commands we may not
rely in every instance on the practices of customary morality or even on the teachings of wise and virtuous men.
A belief in the objectivity of truth carries with it no
assurance of the infallibility of any man or group, anywhere or at any time.

But what appear to me to be much graver embarrassments are inherent in any subjective theory. As Russell
has pointed out, the definition of truth as the opinion
which is fated to be ultimately agreed to by all who investigate "leaves us completely in the dark as to what
the investigators are doing." We can only conclude that,
at the best, they are honest dupes. They conceive themselves to be investigating truth, but actually they are in
the act of creating it by an almost mystical process that
will lead in the end to a "fated" agreement.

Disinterested and high-minded men have said in the

past and men equally disinterested and high-minded will no doubt repeat in the future that the universe in general and life on this planet in particular must be regarded as the results of what may best be described as an accident within an accident—a major and cosmic accident in the first instance and a minor and terrestrial one in the second—and that there is nowhere in the universe intelligence, purpose, or plan. I do not believe it. To the contrary, I have "faith in a universe . . . that has thought and more than thought inside of it"; and I have chosen to record this faith in the form of a quotation. The author of the quotation is Holmes. Here is a fellow wayfarer with whom we thought we had parted company for good and all during the course of our journey. He has rejoined us almost at journey's end, and we must welcome him in accordance with his deserts. I do not profess to know the path that he has followed. It is enough that the greatest of the modern realists came at last to believe not only in Realism but also in Reality.

"O God," exclaimed Kepler in an ecstasy of scientific fervor, "I am thinking Thy thoughts after Thee." The exultation, though reverently expressed, is tinged with a certain unconscious presumption that the modern astronomical physicist will be quick to detect. Men never think God's thoughts after him, but we may nevertheless believe that they possess the capacity for thinking what are, for human purposes at least, reflections and approximations of some of those thoughts. The Christian tradition does not admonish us to approach the fundamental problems of life with a broken and discredited reason, but with a "broken and contrite heart." If Aristotle defended slavery and we denounce it, the lesson to be

〈 124 〉

learned is not that we are wiser than Aristotle, but rather that there is some historical basis for believing that if liberty on the planet survives, the "common law of mankind," like the English common law of which Mansfield spoke, will "work itself pure."

If this faith is groundless, we democrats are of all men most miserable. For we have backed the wrong horse and have bet our lives on a series of propositions that will betray us when they are put to the final test. Of all political forms democracy most needs an ethical system to support it. Men will not go on forever fighting battles whose only objective is victory. They will fight for a cause—for political liberty in a universe in which they believe that moral liberty also exists, for the good life in a universe in which they envisage good and evil as resting on foundations more substantial than human opinion, for the preservation and propagation of truth in a universe in which they have faith to find a power strong enough to make truth-seeking safe and good enough to make truth-telling useful, for the rights of man and the "flag of the world."

In the sense in which I am using the words, government of the people means a government ordained and established by a democratic sovereign. Government by the people means a government either purely democratic or republican in form. Government for the people means a government conducted in accordance with the developing principles of natural justice. If the last is an illusion, or comes generally to be regarded as an illusion, the first and second will surely perish from the earth.

Page 3
Definition of the state. This is a condensation of the definition
of Bentham, which, as Pollock says, is "the foundation of
the modern English [and also American] theory of the state."
History of the Science of Politics, new edition, revised, London, 1935, Macmillan (cited hereafter as *Pollock*), p. 103.
Sometimes, however, "sovereign" and "state" are used as
interchangeable terms. Thus, according to Austin, " 'The
state' is usually synonymous with '*the* sovereign.' It denotes
the individual person, or the body of individual persons, which
bears the supreme power in an independent political society."
Lectures on Jurisprudence, fourth edition, revised and edited
by Campbell, London, 1879, Murray (cited hereafter as
Austin), I, 249, note. And Burgess, repeating the epigram
attributed to Louis XIV, says in discussing the history of the
German Empire that Charlemagne "was sovereign . . . was
the state." *Political Science and Constitutional Law*, Boston
and London, 1890, Ginn (cited hereafter as *Burgess*), I,
109. On the whole, I think it preferable to preserve the distinction between two badly needed words and to use the word
"state" to refer to the aggregate of sovereign and subjects.
If we do so, we may say with at least verbal accuracy that
the France of Louis XIV was a state in which the king was
sovereign, and that the France of the Third Republic was a
state in which the people were sovereign.

Page 4
The publication of a charter. A charter consists of assurances
or promises given by a sovereign to his subjects. Note the accurate style of Magna Carta: "We will sell to no man, we
will deny or delay to no man, either right or justice," etc.

Page 6
Definition of sovereignty. This is paraphrased from *Pollock*,
p. 59. "If," says Austin in an often quoted passage, "a determinate human superior, not in the habit of obedience to a
like superior, receive habitual obedience from the bulk of a

given society, the determinate superior is sovereign in that society, and the society (including the superior) is a society political and independent." *Austin*, I, 226. It seemed to Maine that this definition was expressed "with great concision." Some later writers have been less favorably impressed. In the opinion of Pollock, Austin's manner "is so repulsive . . . that it is hard to be quite just to his matter"; and Professor Mac-Iver thinks that his definition "would turn a pirate ship, a criminal gang, or even a menagerie into a sovereign state." *Pollock*, p. 109, note. MacIver, *Leviathan and the People*, University, Louisiana, 1939, Louisiana State University Press (cited hereafter as *MacIver*), p. 154.

Page 8

Commonwealths. Throughout the text I have used this word in referring to the political subdivisions of the United States *after* the adoption of the Constitution. To call them states would involve an obvious verbal ambiguity.

Page 9

The theory of the absolute sovereign. In presenting this theory I have dealt with only one or two objections. The reader must not conclude, however, that I am ignorant of the fact that other objections to it have been made. I can tolerate all of them except the one most commonly encountered—that the theory is "legalistic." It is the reverse of legalistic. Legalism involves an undue preoccupation with forms, formalities, credentials, and legal procedure. The doctrine of the absolute sovereign ignores all such matters.

Page 10

Things as they ought to be, things as they are supposed to be, and things as they are. If I say that Negroes ought to be allowed to vote in the United States, I am talking morality. If I say that they have the right to vote by virtue of the Fifteenth Amendment, I am talking law. If I say that they are prohibited from voting in many parts of the deep South, I am talking politics. As used here and at other places, the word "supposed" refers to an ostensible or formal status. "The scrubs are not supposed to beat the varsity" does not mean that the boys think that the scrubs never beat the varsity. It means that when they do beat them, the boys recognize that what has happened is outside the expected pattern.

Some writers would amend the statement in the text to read that the science of politics is concerned, *at least in the first instance*, with things as they are. As suggested in the foreword, it seems clearer to me to stick to a narrow definition of politics and to note simply that political philosophers, like nearly everyone else, sometimes give consideration to moral questions.

Page 12

In every government the majority rules. Burke's view was as follows: "In all forms of government the people is the true legislator; and whether the immediate and instrumental cause of the law be a single person or many, the remote and efficient cause is the consent of the people, either actual or implied; and such consent is absolutely essential to its validity." *Burke's Politics,* New York, 1949, Knopf (cited hereafter as *Burke*), p. 151. The comment in the text on the saying of Aristotle is that actual or presently potential power is to be distinguished from remotely potential power. Burke's language requires the further comment that the existence of sovereign power is one thing, and its "validity" something else. I have discussed the opinions of Savigny in Chapter 6. Compare Gray: "The people no more have created and uphold the state because they have the physical strength to kill their rulers, than the horses of a regiment of cavalry have created and uphold the regiment because they have the physical strength to demolish their riders." *The Nature and Sources of the Law,* second edition, New York, 1938, Macmillan (cited hereafter as *Gray*), p. 68.

Page 14

Pericles and Aspasia, and the causes of causes. Conscious persuasion is only one of many causes of causes. "The vast mass of influences, which we may call for shortness moral, perpetually shapes, limits or forbids the actual direction of the forces of society by its Sovereign." Maine expounding Austin in *Early History of Institutions,* New York, 1888, Holt (cited hereafter as *Maine*), p. 359.

⟨ 129 ⟩

Page 21

Holmes's test of truth. The validity of this test is explicitly rejected in the concluding chapter.

Page 21

Thrasymachus. He has had some modern followers. See Treitschke as quoted by Gettell, *History of Political Thought*, New York, 1924, Appleton-Century, p. 432.—"Might is at once the supreme right, and the dispute as to what is right is decided by the arbitrament of war."

Page 25

Laws in which no moral principle is involved. The classic example is the rule of the road. Any rule is better than none. Whether we are to turn to the right or to the left must be determined by custom or legislation; and in fact the rule is not the same in all countries.

Page 25

Influence of morality on the law. Conversely the law exercises a certain influence on morality; but this is so, as Professor Fuller has pointed out, "only because of a kind of tacit presumption that what is 'law' is also, in some sense or other, 'right.' The attitudes which the law thus indirectly shapes derive their sanction, not from their legal origin, but from a public conviction of their 'rightness.' " *The Law in Quest of Itself*, Chicago, 1940, Foundation (cited hereafter as *Fuller*), p. 112.

Page 26

The sentimental error of Cicero and Blackstone. This characterization is entirely fair to Blackstone, whose complacency was limitless. Cicero, however, took notice of the fact that the law does not always command what is right and prohibit what is wrong, and attempted to reckon with the resulting problem.

Page 27

Dissenters from the judgment against Creon. Machiavelli drew a distinction between public and private morality, and hence must probably be included among them.

Page 27

St. Paul and the powers that be. I say that support for the proposition that even the unjust commands of the sovereign

ought to be obeyed has been *sought* in this passage. I do not
profess to know what St. Paul meant, and I do not believe in
torturing texts. However, two comments occur to me: (1)
For obvious reasons he did not intend to take issue with the
saying that we are to render to Caesar the things that are
Caesar's and to God the things that are God's. (2) Since he
submitted to martyrdom rather than commit his conscience
to the keeping of the powers that be, it is clear that if his
words require the interpretation which some writers have
placed upon them, he did not practice what he preached.
Priestley regarded it "a sufficient answer to such an absurd
quotation as [the one in the text] that, for the same reason,
the powers which will be will be ordained of God also."

Page 29

Aquinas, St. Augustine, and others. I have called these witnesses on behalf of Antigone. I agree with their testimony,
though not in very instance with the form in which it is given.
To my thinking nothing but confusion results from arguing
that a law that is not just is "no law at all," or that edicts
contrary to natural justice are "void." It is simpler and more
accurate to say that some laws are good and some bad; and
that if a law is bad enough the duty of the subject is to break it.

Page 30

The usually serene Emerson. I am indebted for the happily
chosen adjective to Morrison and Commager, *The Growth
of the American Republic*, New York, 1942, Oxford University Press, I, 606.

Page 30

The historical argument. For the reasons suggested in the
text the decision of the Supreme Court of the United States
in *United States* v. *Macintosh*, 283 U.S. 605 (now happily
overruled), seems to me the very worst ever handed down
by that court. This case is to be sharply distinguished from
United States v. *Schwimmer*, 279 U.S. 644 (now also overruled), which had been decided about two years previously.
Both cases were concerned with the naturalization of aliens,
and in both of them citizenship was denied. Naturalization is
not a right but a privilege, and in each case the underlying

question, stripped of technicalities, was what sort of persons are likely to make desirable American citizens. Rosika Schwimmer was an uncompromising pacifist, who testified that she would not be willing to bear arms under any circumstances whatever. Conceding the force of what was said by Holmes in dissent, and of much else that might be said, about the contribution which has been made to the United States by the Quakers and other pacifists, I can still see that philosophic pacifism presents a problem in time of war and that the American people, though fully determined to extend toleration to pacifists among their fellow citizens, might consider it inexpedient to add to the number by naturalization. If I had been a member of the court that heard the Schwimmer case, I believe that I would not have voted in accordance with this view; but I do not regard it as altogether unreasonable. But Professor Macintosh was not a pacifist. He was a Canadian by birth, who had sought and obtained appointment as a chaplain in the Canadian army during the First World War and had seen service at the front. He testified only that he would not promise in advance to bear arms in defense of the United States unless he believed the war to be morally justified. Unless I grossly misunderstand the principles of our Constitution, this attitude is not an aberration or eccentricity but is in exact accordance with our most deeply felt political traditions. When the citizens of a democratic state have become so subservient to their government that they will give their lives to it in support of a war that they themselves recognize as iniquitous, it is time to expect the advent of the man on horseback.

Page 31

Wise and foolish martyrs. Dr. Johnson delivered himself on this subject: "Sir, the only method by which religious truth can be established is by martyrdom. The magistrate has a right to enforce what he thinks; and he who is conscious of the truth has a right to suffer. I am afraid there is no other way of ascertaining the truth, but by persecution on the one hand and enduring it on the other. . . . Sir, if a man is in doubt whether it would be better for him to expose himself to martyrdom or not, he should not do it. He must be convinced that he has a delegation from heaven." Boswell's *Life*, London, edition of 1922, Oxford, I, 512. The attentive reader will perhaps notice that in this passage the great lexicographer was not as careful in using the word *right* as he ought to have been. Moreover, we may hope that martyrdom is not the *only* method by which religious truth can be established. But I agree unreservedly that a martyr in doubt had better not be a martyr at all.

Page 39

Rights effective against private persons and rights effective against the government. I call the former simply rights granted *by* the government and the sum total of the latter *civil liberty*. Professor Corwin would take exception to this terminology. "We enjoy *civil liberty*," he says, "because of the restraints which government imposes upon our neighbors in our behalf and *constitutional liberty* because of the constitutional restraints under which government itself operates when it seeks to impose restraints upon us." *Liberty Against Government*, Baton Rouge, 1948, Louisiana State University Press, p. 7. These statements are both clear and logical, but they involve the use of the term *civil liberty* in a sense at variance with its commonly understood meaning. The Germans are a law abiding people, and the German police (I do not refer to secret police) before the first World War were highly efficient. Professor Corwin's definitions would make it necessary for him to describe the subjects of the Kaiser as endowed with as high a degree of civil liberty as has perhaps been found anywhere in the course of recorded history. I must confess that I find this description somewhat startling. It is hardly necessary to point out that the disagreement here is altogether verbal. Professor Corwin and I are talking about precisely the same things, though under different names. *Any* terminology will do if it is accurately explained and consistently followed. I have tried to meet that requirement.

Page 54

No difficulty in English in using republic in Aristotle's good sense; but it has never been done. A republic, according to modern usage, is a form of *government*, not a form of *state*; and it is that form of government "in which the scheme of representation takes place"—i.e., it is to be distinguished from what is sometimes described as a "purely democratic" government. See Madison, *The Federalist*, No. x, New York, 1888, Putnam (cited hereafter as *The Federalist*), p. 57.

Page 66

Theoretical advantages of a democratic government. Rousseau was correct in thinking that where a democratic sovereign has established a democratic government, the conduct of the government will, in most instances, conform to the sovereign's will. Indeed, it is only where the machinery of democracy fails to function properly—e.g., where popularly elected legislators persistently misrepresent the will that they are intended to express—that there need be any direct interference by the sovereign in the business of government. The same thing is true, to a greater or less degree, even in a monarchy or an aristocracy. Not many individual sovereigns (at least in the Western world) have administered justice like Louis IX under the oak at Vincennes. In all forms of state the sovereign sets up the type of government that accords with his wishes and, so long as it functions in the intended manner, lets it alone. He is required to intervene only if his wishes change or if the conduct of the government ceases to accord with his wishes.

Page 66

The two questions to be submitted. Jefferson argued that an occasional revolution (he did not mean by the word a change in sovereigns but an overthrow of the government by the sovereign) was a medicine necessary to the health of the state, and that, apart from revolutions, the fundamental law ought to be revised as a matter of routine at intervals of nineteen years.

Page 68

A sovereign active only once or twice in a century. Compare Green's *Lectures on the Principles of Political Obligation*, London, New York and Toronto, reprint of 1941, Longmans, p. 112: "In the United States, with a written constitution, it required all Austin's subtlety to detect where sovereignty lay, and he places it where probably no ordinary citizen of the United States had ever thought of it as residing, viz. 'in the states' governments as forming one aggregate body: meaning by a state's government, not its ordinary legislature, but the body of citizens which appoints its ordinary legislature, and which, the union apart, is properly sovereign therein.' " This is a needlessly involved way of saying that in the United States sovereignty resides in the whole body of the people (more precisely, in the whole body of the electors). Hardly any American ever thinks of it as residing anywhere else. Pollock concedes (p. 51, note) that "there is no doubt that the weight of American opinion, from the Fathers of the Constitution downwards, ascribes ultimate sovereignty to the people of the United States as a whole."

Page 69

The sovereign and the Zeitgeist. If the Grand Vizier orders your head to be cut off, he seems to exercise sovereign power but he does not really do so. The Sultan may learn about your predicament in time and set you at liberty. In like manner, the House of Commons often looks and acts like the sovereign, though it is only the creature of the electorate. May we take another step and conclude that in a democracy the electorate is itself a representative body and that the true sovereign is the *Zeitgeist?* The answer is no. This is our former case of Pericles and Aspasia. We cannot go beyond the statement in the text. The *Zeitgeist* has no political *power* but it wields enormous political *influence*; and the larger the electorate is in relation to the entire population, the greater its influence becomes. "The greatness of what we call democratic government does not lie in the mere fact that a numerical majority controls at election time, but at a time further removed from the ballot box, in the forces which are permitted to play upon the electorate." *Fuller*, p. 123. Compare *MacIver*, p. 153: "In a democracy the state never sleeps, for public opinion is active all the time, not only as an indirect determinant of governmental policies but as a judge taking evidence on which later to pass judgment."

⟨ 135 ⟩

Page 70

Unanimity, on one occasion at least. Burke is not recorded as having been an admirer of Rousseau. Nevertheless, he agreed with him on this point: "We hear much, from men who have not acquired their hardiness of assertion from the profundity of their thinking, about the omnipotence of a *majority*, in such a dissolution of an ancient society as has taken place in France. But amongst men so disbanded there can be no such thing as majority or minority, or power in any one person to bind another. The power of acting by a majority, which the gentlemen theorists seem to assume so readily, after they have violated the contract out of which it has arisen (if at all it existed), must be grounded on two assumptions: first, that of an incorporation produced by unanimity; and secondly, a unanimous agreement that the act of a mere majority (say of one) shall pass with them and with others as the act of the whole." *Burke*, p. 396.

Page 72

Ireland and India. It seemed to me in my youth that the attitude of the Protestant minority in Ireland was "undemocratic." It may be practically inexpedient or even, *arguendo*, morally wrong; but I have come to think that the adjective undemocratic is inapplicable. As long as the Protestants feel, for whatever reasons, that it would be intolerable to be governed by Catholics, nothing is to be gained by submitting the question to an election at which they would be certain to lose. They have no recourse except to resist. This is what they did, and therefore Ireland is politically divided. I am of a like opinion about the Moslems and Hindus in India.

Page 73

Minority rule as the only alternative to majority rule. Contrast the views of Henry Steele Commager in *Majority Rule and Minority Rights*, New York, 1943, Oxford University Press, with Calhoun's idea of the "concurrent majority" in his *Disquisition on Government*, New York, 1947, reprint of original edition, Political Science Classics. Both sides of the question are well summarized in *MacIver*, pp. 151-153.

Page 74
"Majority rule" itself often minority rule. In the bitterly contested presidential election held in the United States in 1940 the popular vote for all candidates for president was only fifty millions, whereas the population of the United States as shown by the census made in the same year was upwards of 131 millions; and of the fifty millions of electors who went to the polls only twenty-seven millions, or about one-fifth of the population, supported the winning candidate.

Page 74
Lincoln in a famous letter. The letter to Greeley. "My paramount object in this struggle is to save the Union, and is not either to save or to destroy slavery. If I could save the Union without freeing any slave, I would do it; if I could save it by freeing all the slaves, I would do it; and if I could save it by freeing some and leaving others alone, I would also do that."

Page 75
Our history has been a fortunate one. Nevertheless, in its less fortunate aspects it has followed the familiar pattern. The amendments abolishing slavery and providing for Negro suffrage were forcibly added to the Constitution at the conclusion of the Civil War. The first was immediately accepted by the people of the South as an inescapable consequence of military defeat. The second has never been accepted by them and up to the present time has been virtually nullified except in the North, where the consequences of its enforcement are of little moment.

Page 80
The nature and sources of the law. Before attempting a classification of states we were careful to salute the memory of Aristotle. Here a like salutation is due to the memory of Professor John Chipman Gray, whose *Nature and Sources of the Law*, published in 1909 when the author was seventy years old, was the first philosophical exposition of that subject to appear in the United States. As Gray confessed in his disarming preface, "when one has been reading and thinking on a subject for half a century, it is difficult, indeed impos-

sible, to tell what is one's own and what one owes to others."
Certainly, whether for better or worse, I owe a great deal
to him in the preparation of this chapter—not only in the
content and arrangement but also (I suspect) unconsciously
in the style. In spite of this heavy indebtedness, I have been
led to reject his principal conclusion—namely, that all law
is made by the courts.

Page 81

Runjeet Singh. The quotation is from *Maine*, p. 380. Maine
was quite right in saying that this despotic chieftain never
made a law. The point is well illustrated in the *Book of
Esther.* In the first instance, Ahasuerus, influenced by the
wicked Haman, issued an order commanding his lieutenants
and governors to kill all the Jews in his dominions. Afterwards, when the perfidy of Haman had been established,
Esther implored the king to "reverse" this order; but he felt
himself unable to comply on the ground that a "writing which
is written in the king's name, and sealed with the king's ring,
may no man reverse." Consequently, he issued a second
order, warning the Jews of the first one and commanding
them to defend themselves—a somewhat costly method of
correcting a mistake. It is clear that Ahasuerus had no idea
of the meaning of "law in the lawyer's sense." The "laws"
that could not be changed were simply ukases or decrees to
meet specific emergencies.

Page 86

*The difference between the relationship of law and custom
in a democracy and in any other form of state.* Compare
Austin's criticism (ii, pp. 557-558) of a passage in Julian to
the effect that "a customary rule which the people actually
observes, is equivalent to a law which the people establishes
formally; since the people (*which is the sovereign*) is the immediate author of each." As Austin justly observes, "ad-
mitting that the position will hold, *where the people is the
sovereign,* how can the position possibly apply, where the people
is ruled by an oligarchy, or where it is subject to a monarch?
There, laws, established formally by the sovereign one or
few, are not established by the subject many. And, on the

other hand, customs observed spontaneously by the subject people, are not the production of the monarch, or of the sovereign body."

Page 87

Savigny's doctrines applicable only and even then not universally to what law ought to be in any state and is supposed to be in a democracy. The original statutes requiring the vaccination of school children were not declaratory of an existing practice. They were adopted by the legislature at the instance of a small number of scientists and physicians. We must suppose, however, that there was a popular demand for the control of smallpox. A compliance, doubtless unwilling in the first place, with the requirements of the statutes entailed no more than a trifling inconvenience and expense and resulted in a striking decrease in the prevalence of smallpox. Hence a practice was initiated that would now be followed by most parents in the absence of any statute.

Page 89

Osric and Horatio. The language in the text is an interesting example of unconscious plagiarism. In Professor Toynbee's *A Study of History* there is a reference to the racial theory of civilization "which sets upon a pedestal the xanthotrichous, glaucopian, dolichocephalic variety of *homo leucodermaticus,* called by some the Nordic man and by Nietzsche 'the blond beast.'" In Mr. Somervell's abridgment of the first six volumes of Professor Toynbee's work, New York and London, 1947, Oxford, p. 52, the following footnote to this passage appears: " 'Is't not possible to understand in another tongue?' asks Horatio. It is: to wit, 'yellow-haired, grey-eyed, longheaded variety of white-skinned man.' " Mr. Somervell will have to take my word for it that I had written my sentences before I saw his.

Page 98

Sole and express purpose of revising the Articles of Confederation. Eleven states were represented when this resolution was adopted. See Bloom, *The Story of the Constitution,* Washington, 1937, U. S. Sesquicentennial Commission, p. 17.

Page 100

A sovereign nation of many sovereign states. It is a pity
that this foolish phrase has been embedded in the mosaic
known as *The American Creed.* *"Credo quia impossibile"* is
not a sound maxim in politics.

Page 102

When did this shift of sovereignty take place? Professor
Corwin in his essay *"We, the People"* in *The Doctrine of
Judicial Review,* Princeton, 1914, Princeton University
Press, p. 81, has assembled an impressive body of evidence
tending to show that it was generally believed by the founding fathers and others at the time of, and immediately after,
the ratification of the Constitution that the effect of ratification was to vest sovereignty in the people of the United States
as a whole. Of course this opinion was not *universally* held.
The Kentucky Resolutions, which were drafted by Jefferson,
begin with the declaration that "the several *States* composing
the United States of America . . . by a *compact* under the
style and title of a Constitution for the United States . . . constituted a general government for special purposes." In any
event, Professor Corwin and I are not dealing with the same
problem. His question is: What did the founding fathers *think*
they were doing? The question propounded in the text is, in
effect: What would have *happened* if South Carolina had
attempted to secede, say, fifty years before Fort Sumter was
fired on? An answer is at least suggested by what did happen
when secession was threatened in 1832. However, Jackson
was an exceptionally vigorous President, and the event might
have been different with another man in the White House.
For whatever reason, the threatened attempt was not made.
My question lies in the realm of speculation, and, as I say
in the text, no final answer to it can be given.

In *Texas* v. *White,* 7 Wallace 700 (1869), Chief Justice
Chase presented what seems at first sight to be still another
interpretation of the facts. He said: "The Union of the States
never was a purely artificial and arbitrary relation. It began
among the Colonies, and grew out of common origin, mutual
sympathies, kindred principles, similar interests, and geograph-

ical relations. It was confirmed and strengthened by the necessities of war, and received definite form, and character, and sanction from the Articles of Confederation. By these the Union was solemnly declared to 'be perpetual.' And when these Articles were found to be inadequate to the exigencies of the country, the Constitution was ordained 'to form a more perfect Union.' It is difficult to convey the idea of indissoluble unity more clearly than by these words. What can be indissoluble if a perpetual Union, made more perfect, is not?"

This, I think, is a piece of legalism, though one that was perhaps justified by the condition of the country at the time it was announced. Nobody can deny that there was a "union" of the states before either the Constitution or the Articles of Confederation. On the other hand, nobody can deny that this union was originally confederate in form and that any member had both the right and the power to withdraw from it, and that afterwards it was made to appear that the union had become federal in form and that no member had the power to withdraw. The Chief Justice went on to say that "the Constitution . . . looks to an indestructible Union composed of indestructible States." The legalism is particularly daring here because, whatever the Constitution may be held to "look to," the writer had himself seen the "indestructible" state of Virginia destroyed by being divided in two against the wishes of a majority of its inhabitants. Of course, criticism of this sort was current at the time the opinion was delivered. Mr. Justice Grier protested in his dissenting opinion that the question on which the case turned—whether Texas was a member of the Union—had been decided on the basis of "a legal fiction" rather than "a political fact," and argued that the court was "bound to know and notice the public history of the nation." A political writer, at all events, is bound by that obligation. In my view, however, the significant political fact is not that Texas attempted to secede but that the attempt was defeated by force of arms.

⟨ 141 ⟩

Page 106

No similar like-mindedness prevails throughout the world today. It does prevail, however, among the members of the English-speaking peoples. Since, in addition, these states are all democratic, the formation of a federal union embracing all of them presents no theoretical difficulties. If the requisite popular support for it were obtained, there is no reason why it could not be carried out.

Page 108

Peace and righteousness. Compare Kant, who, though he taught that resistance to the Head of the State was the worst of crimes, nevertheless declared: "If justice perishes it is of no value any longer that man live on the earth." See Catlin, *The Story of the Political Philosophers*, New York, 1947, Tudor, p. 416.

Page 112

Democratic pessimists. Professor Kelsen must be included. "The idea underlying the principle of majority is that the social order shall be in concordance with as many subjects as possible, and in discordance with as few as possible. Since political freedom means agreement between the individual will and the collective will expressed in the social order, it is the principle of simple majority which secures the highest degree of political freedom that is possible within society." *General Theory of Law and State*, Cambridge, 1945, Harvard University Press, p. 286. At the worst, fifty-one per cent of the subjects are happy and only forty-nine per cent are miserable.

Page 114

Holmes in praise of Montesquieu. The passage quoted in the text seems to me to contain an error in logic as well as in philosophy. If "the proximate test of a good government is that the dominant power has its way," all governments are good and anarchy is the only political evil. If the dominant power did not have its way, it would not be dominant.

Page 118

Natural law. Professor Kelsen thinks that this doctrine is anarchistic in tendency. Doubtless the criticism is correct, but

I am not disturbed by it. A philosophic anarchist seems to me a much more respectable figure than a totalitarian.

Page 119

Suppose it to be demonstrated, etc. This illustration is paraphrased from one given by Brecht in "Beyond Relativism in Political Theory," an article published in the *American Political Science Review*, June, 1947, p. 475.

Page 120

The many more merciful than the one or the few. Compare Froude, *Caesar: a Sketch*, New York, 1879, Scribner, p. 85: ". . . Impartial history declares . . . that the crimes of the popular party have in all ages been the lighter in degree, while in themselves they have more to excuse them; and if the violent acts of revolutionists have been held up more conspicuously for condemnation, it has been only because the fate of noblemen and gentlemen has been more impressive to the imagination than the fate of the peasant or the artisan."

Page 120

Holmes and Mr. Wu. The particular act of faith with which Holmes began was deciding that he was not God. Does this decision imply that there is a God? I leave the answer to the logicians.

Page 121

Cosmic impiety. Russell's warning is the more striking because he cannot be classified as philosophically or theologically orthodox.

Page 122

The sovereign coercing the investigators. This is exactly what Hitler did to scientific thought in Germany, and exactly what the rulers of the Soviet Union are now doing to scientific thought in Russia. If a popular majority in a democratic state adopted the same philosophy, the danger would be equally great.

Page 122

Difficulties in any theory of natural law. Fuller would add to those noticed in the text "an inner aversion to what may look like a claim to oracular powers." He concludes, however: "Strong as this aversion may be, the scholar should remember that while he hesitates to assume a role bearing too unsavory a resemblance to that of the priest in primitive society the time may come when that role is no longer open to him, for we must recall that when the priest abdicates it is generally the warrior and spellbinder who take over." *Fuller*, p. 127.

Page 123

Russell on Peirce's definition of truth. I can see no difference between this definition and that of Holmes except that Holmes spoke of "a present or imagined future *majority* in favor of our view," whereas, according to Peirce, "*all* who investigate" will ultimately agree.

Page 124

Holmes and a universe with thought inside of it. I say in the text that I do not know the path that he followed to arrive at this faith, but I agree with Professor Fuller that "his very inconsistencies made him a more effective advocate of the positivistic philosophy than such men as Austin and Kelsen, who never let the green fields of life lure them from the gray path of logic." *Fuller*, p. 118.

Page 124

Kepler and God's thoughts. A distinguished scientific friend of mine has said that "the Euclid-Newton bank honored all the drafts that were drawn on it for upwards of two hundred years." Nevertheless, in our own generation the bank has begun to dishonor drafts.

INDEX OF PROPER NAMES